# GOD
## IS GREAT AND I AM GRATEFUL

# TONY PEAK

*For with GOD nothing shall be impossible. Luke 1:37*

# GOD IS GREAT AND I AM GRATEFUL

The Story of a Miracle-Working God and the Incredible Rescue of a *Covid-19 Victim*

**CEDAR GATE**
**PUBLISHING**

Copyright © 2023 Tony Peake

ISBN13: 979-8986943893

All rights reserved. No part of this book may be reproduced or transmitted in any form or by any means, electronic or mechanical, including photocopying and recording, or by an information storage and retrieval system, without permission in writing from the author.

# Table of Contents

SECTION I IN THE BEGINNING . . . . . . . . . . . . . . . 17

CHAPTER 1 Ground Zero . . . . . . . . . . . . . . . . . . . . . . 19

SECTION II MEET ME IN SHAWNEE . . . . . . . . . 23

CHAPTER 2 Covid Lands the First Blow . . . . . . . . . . 25

CHAPTER 3 Merry Christmas! . . . . . . . . . . . . . . . . . . 37

CHAPTER 4 Happy New Year, Maybe! . . . . . . . . . . . . 43

SECTION III OKLAHOMA CITY LOOKS,
OH, SO PRETTY . . . . . . . . . . . . . . . . . . . . . . . . . . . . 47

CHAPTER 5 For Better or for Worse . . . . . . . . . . . . . . 49

CHAPTER 6 Go Ahead, Make My Day . . . . . . . . . . . . 61

CHAPTER 7 A Friend that Sticks Closer
Than a Brother. . . . . . . . . . . . . . . . . . . . . . . . . . . . . . 65

CHAPTER 8 Gonna Make It . . . . . . . . . . . . . . . . . . . . 75

CHAPTER 9 Major Pain. . . . . . . . . . . . . . . . . . . . . . . . 83

CHAPTER 10 Beauty for Ashes . . . . . . . . . . . . . . . . . . 89

CHAPTER 11 Looking Good! . . . . . . . . . . . . . . . . . . . 97

CHAPTER 12 Large and in Charge . . . . . . . . . . . . . . 103

CHAPTER 13 Keep Your Eye on the Prize. . . . . . . . . 115

CHAPTER 14 Give and It Will Be Given . . . . . . . . . . 125

SECTION IV BUZZING OFF TO THE BEE. . . . . . 131

CHAPTER 15 Jehovah Jireh . . . . . . . . . . . . . . . . . . . . 133

CHAPTER 16 Reserve Your Place . . . . . . . . . . . . . . . . 141

CHAPTER 17 Do You Want to Get Well? . . . . . . . . . . 147

CHAPTER 18 Praise the Lord! . . . . . . . . . . . . . . . . . . 153

CHAPTER 19 Cry Me A River…And Laugh
Me One Too . . . . . . . . . . . . . . . . . . . . . . . . . . . . . . . 161

CHAPTER 20 Step by Step . . . . . . . . . . . . . . . . . . . . . 171

CHAPTER 21 Great Is Thy Faithfulness . . . . . . . . . . . 177

CHAPTER 22 - "The Surreal Deal" . . . . . . . . . . . . . . . 191

CHAPTER 23 The Pathway to Victory . . . . . . . . . . . . 203

CHAPTER 24 Down the Home Stretch . . . . . . . . . . . 209

ACKNOWLEDGEMENTS . . . . . . . . . . . . . . . . . . . 237

# FOREWORD

The day was June 7, 2003, at First Baptist Church of Tecumseh, and I was marrying Jill Evans. Jill had been in Tony Peak's youth group, and his influence on her formative years, his friendship with her family over the years, and his clear heart for Christ made him the obvious officiant for the occasion. Tony began his remarks outlining his long association with Jill and her family. He then turned toward me and said something to the effect of, "I have not gotten to know Justin very well, but I understand he is a St. Louis Cardinals fan, so he must be alright."

That was it. That was his endorsement, and that was our commonality.

It has been six thousand, nine hundred and ninety-two days since that first encounter and the establishment of our friendship. Our bond is stronger and our commonalities more numerous, though that first one about the Cardinals still comes up often.

For the past several years, we have met monthly to eat together, share life together, and pray together. It was for that reason I texted with Tony in November of 2020. He texted back that he had tested positive for COVID and would not be able to meet. As Thanksgiving came and went, Tony would get more sick and end up in the hospital. We would not have our regular lunches again until August of 2021. On that day, I would eat my lunch on Tony's couch, and he would lie in his hospital bed and sip on a chocolate Ensure.

This book details the events in between and the God-sent people that Tony crossed paths with along the way. Within those events, Tony shows us what we all can learn about God and our relationship with Him through Jesus Christ. Tony plainly states his goals in sharing his story. He simply and deeply wants to honor the God that has been with him not just through the last two years but his whole life.

Tony believes that God wants him to share his story because you need to know it. Not that you need to know what Tony has done, but you need to know what it means to be grateful no matter what. You need to have your view of God expanded because God's greatness is boundless. Tony has done what the Holy Spirit has prompted him to do, and he has done it in a way that pulls you in and forces you to ask questions that will lead to freeing answers. Even in times of great trial, great pain, and great frustration, God is great. I am grateful for Tony. I am grateful that he is here today. I am grateful that his faithfulness has and will continue to affect real people in real life.

I invite you to read and pray through this book. As you do, I hope that you feel better. I am not talking about an emotional feeling, but a whole body, whole spirit feeling. The God who made you loves you, period. We discover what it means through God's truth, our stories, and others' stories. Tony has lovingly poured out his story because it points to our great, loving God. I am grateful that he has, and I think you will be, too.

Dr. Justin Dunn, Pastor

University Baptist Church

July 29, 2022

# INTRODUCTION

As pastor of First Baptist Church, in Tecumseh, Oklahoma, in November of 2021, I was visiting the home of Debra Fletcher, one of my church members. Debra is a committed Christian (should there be any other kind?), an unceasing prayer warrior, and a darn good baker. Her chocolate and strawberry cupcakes are to die for. In our conversation, Debra tells me, "You should write a book about your experiences with Covid." Something about her comment struck a nerve. A good nerve, but a scary nerve.

My experiences with Covid-19 that Debra spoke of included 193 days in five hospitals and several months of rehabbing after being released.

Others would make the same suggestion to me and to my wife, Alicia. "Tony really ought to write a book." With that, I committed to pray about the possibility of writing about our journey through Covid. But in my prayers, I gave God my best impression of Moses at the burning bush, offering one excuse after another as to why I couldn't write a book. Chuck Swindoll, David Jeremiah, Tony Evans, Max Lucado, Priscilla Shirer are authors. Who am I to believe I could author a book?

I thought I had God stopped dead cold when I prayed, "And

another thing, Lord, writing a book would require lots of time, time I just don't have now." Case closed. End of story and book writing.

Then came Sunday, February 20, 2022. During the previous week, Alicia and I had made the decision that it was time for us to leave our ministry at First Baptist Church in Tecumseh. So, I read my letter of resignation at the conclusion of the morning service that day.

About Tuesday of my first week after resigning, the Holy Spirit whispered in my ear, "How about that book now, Tony? You have nothing BUT time." Busted. It is always good when the Holy Spirit gets to have His way in your life, but it isn't always easy to swallow.

I spent the next few days allowing God to adjust my attitude. I had done some writing before, but I had never tackled anything as enormous as writing a book. It was a "David versus Goliath" thing, and I was David. David was obedient and bold. So I needed to be as well. I summoned up all of my moxie and proclaimed to my giant called Fear, "You come at me with doubt and dread, but I come at you in the name of the Lord ... and my HP laptop!"

So, here it is. The result of that surrender. "God is Great and I Am Grateful." This entire project is dedicated to proclaiming how great is our wonderful and wonder-working Lord who literally delivered me from the jaws of death multiple times and nurtured me through a lengthy and painful recovery from the effects of Covid-19. First and foremost, we serve a merciful and gracious God who never runs out of wonders. Quoting Cindy Bradley, one dear sister in Christ, when it comes to God's working, "I am never surprised, but always amazed!"

I hope to glorify Him by sharing this story of His work in the lives of Alicia and I during the darkest days of our lives together. In times in the hospital when I was discouraged, Alicia would remind me, "God hasn't brought us this far to let us go." And she was right.

Unfortunately or fortunately, I have little to no memory of the first six to eight weeks. So I decided to begin writing from the stories, journals, and Facebook posts of my wife, Alicia. I've included many excerpts taken directly from her journal & Facebook (you'll find those entries throughout the book in italics).

And through this story, may you discover a nugget of faith, a renewed confidence, a refreshed spirit, an enduring hope that will help you gain victory over whatever Covid-sized-like battle you are facing. May Galatians 6:9 be your battle cry, "And let us not be weary in well doing for in due season we will reap, if we faint not." (KJV)

There is no substitute for getting started. And on the day I started writing, I first wrote this personal declaration.

> **I have no idea what I am doing, but I know for Whom I am doing it. Today, March 21, 2022, I begin to put down words of what I hope to be a book that glorifies God and displays His magnificence.**
>
> *Lord, I dedicate this work to you. I do this only because I feel you have called me to it. Help me as I try to be faithful to your call. Give me counsel where I need counsel. Give me encouragement when I am discouraged. Give me victory by seeing this project*

*through to its completion. In Jesus name, Amen.*

In 2007, Christopher Hitchens authored "God Is Not Great." But my experiences over the last year and a half leads me to no other conclusion than God IS great. Buckle up and enjoy the ride in "God Is Great and I Am Grateful."

*"Covid is a beast without a heart. It has no compassion. The beast will strike anybody, and it doesn't matter to it who it leaves dead along the way."*

(Quote by author in an interview with KWTV reporter, Barry Mangold, August 21, 2021)

# DEDICATION

This book is dedicated to the hard-working and committed health care professionals battling Covid still today, to all the prayer warriors who waged war on their knees for Alicia and me, to Alicia, my wonderful and supportive wife, and to a great God to whom I am forever grateful.

# SECTION I

# IN THE BEGINNING

# CHAPTER 1

## Ground Zero

Saturday, November 14, 2020, stands out in my mind for two reasons. First, I recall it as the day I traveled from my home in Tecumseh, Oklahoma, to the site near Medford, Oklahoma, where my friend, Richard Bailey, had graciously provided a spot for me to deer hunt. The deer rifle season in Oklahoma would open the following Saturday, and I was going to set up my ground blind and corn feeder in advance.

This year's hunt would be special. My six-year-old grandson, Jordy, had asked if he could go hunting with me for the first time. I thought about it for a nanosecond and said, "You bet!" I purchased a new ground blind (which is basically a small camouflage tent with windows on all sides) big enough to accommodate both of us. And to give us even more space inside the blind, I purchased smaller, three-legged chairs. I also was replacing my defunct corn feeder with a brand-new model.

The temperature was mild for November and there was a steady breeze blowing from the south. I remember the direction of the wind because I had to pull my truck up to the south side of where I wanted to erect my ground blind and use the truck as a windbreak.

You haven't lived until you have tried to accomplish this feat in the Oklahoma wind (which comes sweeping down the plains). It is like trying to fly a giant camouflage kite.

I finally got the blind set up and did the same with the corn feeder, adjusting the timer to automatically deliver exactly the right amount of corn at exactly the right time each day. With the job completed, I motored the two-and-a-half-hour trip back home, and spent the week in anticipation of the upcoming hunt.

That Saturday was also significant because it would be the last thing I would remember until late January 2021. Here unfolds God's story of His greatness and my gratitude for His deliverance of my very life.

On Sunday, November 15, I preached at my church, First Baptist Church of Tecumseh and headed home for Sunday dinner. I mentioned to Alicia that I wasn't feeling well. At this time, America was in the first year of Covid-19 pandemic panic, so if someone got as much as a runny nose or a paper cut, it was off to get a Covid test.

The next day, I drove myself to nearby Shawnee to be tested. Bingo! On Tuesday, November 17, I got the results showing I tested positive for Covid. So I hunkered down to wait out the virus and the mandatory quarantine period.

The following seven days would be a roller coaster of stomach issues, accelerating fatigue, fever, loss of appetite (not normal for a 229 pound chow hound), dehydration, difficulty breathing, and a couple of trips to the Emergency Room.

Those would turn out to be the better days of my ordeal. The evening of Tuesday, November 24, I collapsed in the floor of our home, conscious but incoherent. Alicia called Kay Jordan, an APRN and former member of our youth group in my youth ministry days. On my cell phone, Alicia took a call from Chris Carpenter, our primary care APRN, who was calling to check up on me.

With Kay on one phone and Chris on the other, Alicia heard them both say she needed to call 911 for an ambulance and get me to the emergency room.

That evening would begin a 193-day journey through five different hospitals.

# SECTION II

# MEET ME IN SHAWNEE

# CHAPTER 2

## Covid Lands the First Blow

*The Encouragement of Faithful Prayer Warriors*

Shawnee is the hub town of Pottawatomie County with a population of about 30,000 happy Okies, in the central portion of Oklahoma. It is the home of the Shawnee High School Wolves, Oklahoma Baptist University Bison, and the final home of Dr. Brewster Higley, who composed the lyrics of the old cowboy tune, "Home on the Range." But yours truly was an old cowboy now stabled in the SSM Hospital in Shawnee and a long way from going home to any range.

Friday, November 27, I was rushed into the intensive care unit due to a highly increased struggle to breath. That evening I had to be intubated (the insertion of a tube into a patient's body, in this case, to achieve artificial ventilation into the trachea). Alicia received a phone call about 5:00 p.m. from Nurse Andrea Jones alerting her that my condition had grown critical, and my chance of survival was slim.

Nurse Andrea told Alicia she was placing the phone up to my ear and she needed to talk to me. She gave the admonition to Alicia that she "was to put on her big girl voice and show no fear" as she spoke to me. So with a heart that was terrified, Alicia put on her best big girl voice and sang to me and prayed with me. The end result was a much calmer patient with reduced labored breathing.

The next few days would be a trying cycle of flipping me from lying on my back to lying on my chest. This process is known as "proning." Early Covid treatments had found some success in this process as being facedown seemed to make breathing easier and to take pressure off the lungs. But it required that I basically be medically paralyzed to prevent movement which could disturb the tube down my throat and create all kinds of damage.

The next few days were a volleyball game (with me as the volleyball), going back and forth trying to balance the percentage of assisted breathing through the ventilator to deliver the best level of oxygen saturation in my lungs. Today I can spit out those facts like I invented the ventilator system, but in those early days I knew nothing about them, and nothing about anything else as I continued my drug-induced amnesia phase.

By now Alicia was in full Covid-19 quarantine thanks to me. I'm such a sharing, caring kind of guy. She would spend the Thanksgiving holiday alone enjoying food brought to her by Terry O'Rorke, a good and caring friend, from the Tecumseh Community Thanksgiving Dinner. Dinner had been sponsored by Randy and Suzanne Gilbert, local business owners.

Meanwhile, I was spending Thanksgiving with my fantastic pulmonologist, Dr. Tony Haddad. Dr. Haddad continued the flip-flop drill of proning. For my protection I had to basically be put in a state of paralysis so that I wouldn't twist the tube down in my throat and harm myself.

*Monday, November 28*

"Dr. Tony (as he is affectionately known) said if my Tony continues to improve, then hopefully only one or two more days being flipped back and forth. Then he will only have to be sedated, not paralyzed while on his stomach. When his O2 level is down to around thirty percent, they will start talking about taking him off of the vent."

Alicia would be asked by Nurse Marcy, if she would like to FaceTime with me.

Those were the days when hospital visitation was practically non-existent due to the pandemic, so FaceTiming was the next best thing.

*Monday, November 28 (again)*

"His face was relaxed even with all the tubes. It was so great to see his face. I was able to talk and pray over him. Marcy said he could hear me, even though he was sedated."

During this period some of our compassionate church members delivered gift cards to the nurses. They also provided radios for each ICU room so music from K-LOVE Christian radio could be played for patients. Meanwhile Alicia would test positive for Covid-19 on Tuesday, December 1, and experience what she described as a three-to-four-day sinus infection-like episode. Covid is an odd duck creating symptoms as mild as loss of smell and taste all the way to a trip to the morgue.

*Thursday, December 2nd*

*Dr. Brozowski explained our situation like this. Covid comes in and stays for a while, then when it gets ready to leave, it sets the house on fire. My fire was just a stove top burner. Tony has a Colorado wildfire burning. He is working his way out of ICU but is still very sick. Bacterial pneumonia has set in.*

December 2nd was a big day in our family that neither Alicia nor I would be able to celebrate. Our daughter, Kaitlyn, and husband, Jack, were going to court to officially adopt and welcome their new daughter, Jaybea Alice, into our family.

Later that day, Alicia would be contacted by Nurse Sherri who would get Alicia connected with me for another FaceTime visit, albeit a one-sided conversation. Sherri left the room and allowed Alicia to talk to me, pray, and read scripture.

I don't know what she read to me that night, but I think Psalm 46:1-3 would have been appropriate, "God is our refuge and strength, an ever-present help in trouble. Therefore we will not fear, though the earth gives way and the mountains fall into the heart of the sea, though its waters roar and foam and the mountains quake with their surging." (NIV)

As you read this, are your waters roaring and foaming and your mountains quaking? My primary purpose in writing this book is to glorify our magnificent God. He is great and greatly to be praised. But I also hope that you find hope in these pages. Covid gets all the headlines today, but all types of headaches and heartaches attack people and abound like June bugs around a porch light on a summer's evening.

Need a little comfort, a little encouragement? Look no farther than the truth of the old hymn which begs us to:

> **Have faith in God**
>
> **He's on his throne**
>
> **Have faith in God**
>
> **He watches o'er his own**
>
> **He cannot fail**
>
> **He must prevail**
>
> **Have faith in God, have faith in God.**

This isn't just a song to be sung in quaint little country churches on Sunday mornings. This is bedrock foundation of truth for the believer. Don't believe anything less than this. Satan's storms and life's lunacy can drive you straight to the edge of despair. Whatever is your condition, there is a God who is positioned to pull you through it.

Sunday, December 6, brought a big nosedive in my flight through Covid. This

would be the second occasion when Alicia was told I wasn't going to survive.

*December 6*

*Tony is hanging in there. He is still on 100% oxygen needed. They aren't sure what caused the nosedive this morning. They did add more antibiotics. All vitals are stable, and he is back on his stomach. Pray, pray, pray.*

On that evening Brandi Burks, a former member of our youth group when I was youth minister at First Baptist,

Tecumseh, posted this announcement on Facebook.

> "Brother Tony has always been there through the years for family, friends, and church members to sit at the hospital, pray for them and pray with them. Now is our turn to show love and support to him and his family. Tomorrow, Monday, we will meet on the west side of the hospital at 6:15 p.m. remaining in our cars, and praying for Tony and the medical staff caring for him and others. Also, we will be lifting up support for Alicia and their family. At 6:30 p.m. we will all blink our headlights, flashlights, phones, and anything else that lights up in support of all of them."

The evening of December 7 delivered quite a sight in the SSM west parking lot. At 6:15 p.m., car after car containing members of our church and our community gathered for a prayer vigil. Nurse Lindsey parted the curtains of my ICU room so the prayer warriors below could see the location of my room on the third floor of the hospital. At 6:30 p.m., car lights and hazard flashers lit up the night. Other nurses began to peer out other windows in the ICU. Nurse Andrea would say, "There wasn't a dry eye in the house".

If you want to demonstrate true, gut-level love for someone, pray. Simply and diligently pray.

On Wednesday, December 8, my heartbeat began to race like a Formula One racecar at Indy. The next day, the staff asked Alicia's permission to shock my heart in an attempt to slow down the heart rate. My previously healthy heart was experiencing atrial fibrillation, also known as AFIB. I guess the shocking treatment was successful. I'm still here!

On Thursday, December 10, my kidneys weren't pumping fluid and had become swollen. Dr. Demarin prescribed Lasix in an effort to help my kidneys.

*Thursday, December 10*

*The only thing predictable about Covid is it is unpredictable.*

So would be the lives of Alicia and me for months to come.

Nurse Sherri and Nurse Lindsey (who is a physical beast in the local gym, by the way) would continue to connect Alicia to my bedside through FaceTime. Then came a big day, Thursday, December 10, Day 17 of "Tony Held Hostage." Alicia was allowed to visit me in my room. Her time would be spent looking at my whiskered face and all the tubing stuck in just about every orifice of my body, but it was good stuff to her. I opened my eyes, and she asked me to blink if I could feel her squeezing my hand. I blinked. It was the biggest, best wink in the history of winks!

The next few days were a chess match trying to get the ventilation percentages and oxygen saturation percentages in sync in hopes of getting me off the ventilator. On Friday, December 18, this Pillsbury Doughboy was down from 229 pounds to 194 pounds.

By Saturday, December 19, Dr. Tony had decided putting in a trach tube and feeding tube was best for my near future. At that point I couldn't hold up my head. But on Sunday, December 20, I was treated by lowering the sedation on me so I could see the Dallas Cowboy game. The Cowboys defeated the San Francisco 49ers, 41-33. Good medicine.

Perhaps here lies a little wisdom. In the AT&T Stadium in Dallas, Texas, two NFL teams squared off for an afternoon of pushing and shoving, grunting and groaning, sweating and swearing, unaware that two hundred miles to the north, a Covid-struck patient was battling hard for better days. And how could they know? Here is the wisdom. You just don't know what everyone is going through on any given day. Therefore, it is a good personal policy to give folks the benefit of the doubt on their behavior, take a pass on judging their attitudes, demonstrate some compassion for a brother or sister that is "getting high on getting by" as the great theologians of the group Asleep at the Wheel used to crone. Proverbs 11:25 nails it for us, "A generous person will prosper; whoever refreshes others will be refreshed." (NIV) Daily freshen up your refreshing skills for those who would need refreshing.

On Monday, December 21, Dr. Tony explains to Alicia that my lack of movement is due to something called *polyneuro myopathy*. It is nerve damage caused by the effects of a severe illness. He reassures her that it can be reversed, but it will take a long time. The rate of recovery is something akin to draining a fifty-five-gallon drum of molasses through a hole one-eighth of an inch in diameter.

The nurses played a cat and mouse game trying to lower my sedation level in preparation for surgery. Too low and the muscles began to be overworked. Too high and, well, it is too high (One shouldn't overthink these things).

On Tuesday, December 23, polyneuro myopathy be darned, I wiggled my feet and toes. No one could explain why.

Maybe there was a snappy tune playing on K-LOVE and I just wanted to dance (shameful stuff for a Baptist preacher).

Wednesday, December 23, arrived and so did my date with the surgeon, Dr. Ian Cassady. Tech Mosha was with me before surgery while I struggled from breathing-induced panic. Mosha called Alicia and over the phone Alicia began to sing and pray with me and gave me a little "do-better" speech. To the amazement of Mosha, I calmed down better than with the administration of any drug.

Surgery to insert a trach tube and a feeding tube went well. Dr. Tony laid out the post-op plan. In twenty-four hours I would begin using my feeding tube for daily nutrition. Not biscuits and gravy, but a guy takes what he can get (Did I mention my fighting weight was down to 177 pounds now? Who loses weight in December?). On Thursday, the sedation level would be dropped again. And last, but not least, I would begin to be weaned off ventilation an hour at a time.

Christmas Eve would come and go with no major changes except for the fact that I wouldn't be at church that night to help conduct the Christmas Eve Service. Christmas wouldn't be the same without a candlelight singing of "Silent Night." Then again, nothing would be the same this Christmas.

That day also brought a moving text-message prayer sent to Alicia. It was offered by Brandi Burks, the former youth group member who earlier sent out the announcement concerning the parking lot prayer vigil. I will let you read an excerpt of it for yourself while I go get more tissues for my upcoming tears.

*Father in heaven,*

*You are holy. You are righteous. You are enough for me. I praise you in all seasons. I worship you for you have always been faithful to me. I know your promises are true. I know you will not turn away from me. I know you hear me when I pray to you. Today I pray asking for your will to be done in the life of one that is precious to me. I pray asking for your healing and deliverance from a terrible disease that has swept over this nation and is bringing heartbreak and fear, isolation and destruction to the lives of those here in America and the world.*

*I thank you for the life of Tony and the great impact he has had in shaping me. I thank you for the guidance he has given to me and for the teaching of your Word that he has poured into my life. What a great man of your Word and a great follower of you he is. His influence is forever on my life. Thank you for calling him and using him and allowing him to touch my life in such a profound way. Your word tells me that he is precious in your sight just as he is mine. I know you love him and hold him in your hands.*

*This morning I am asking that you deliver him from this disease. I call out to you asking that it be cast away and that a true and total miracle would be granted to restore Tony. I pray that your breath fill his lungs this morning in a supernatural way. I ask that you give him a peace and a comfort that wraps around him and strengthens him for this physical battle against this disease. Lord, I ask for your hand of guidance over the doctors, nurses and staff who have been sent to help. I pray for your wisdom to fill them. I ask that you go before them in every situation. Open their eyes to the needs he has and let them be responsive to any critical areas they may not otherwise notice. May they be directed by your divine hand to minister to Tony and help to restore health to his body.*

*Father this disease causes us to be separated from those we love. My heart breaks this morning as I think of so many who have to be alone during this time of illness and battle. I ask that you stand against this disease and give supernatural protection to your people. Your peace and constant calm is needed now Lord. I ask that you give emotional comfort to Tony as he fights this with your help. Father, help him to know your presence. Please give him revelation and direction during this time that he would be healed and then use that healing to restore others' faith in you. Please give comfort to Alicia as she is alone and worried. I ask that your word be the light upon her path Lord. Please give her revelation and true and clear confidence that you are in control and hold all things so perfectly.*

*Father above all things I ask that salvation be brought to those lost and without you. I know this would be and is the cry of Tony's heart today. Whatever it is that this day brings, may it bring glory to you and may it direct lost sheep to you, their shepherd.*

*This morning I am thankful that you hear my cries, you know my heartbreak, and you love your children. May I accept your plan and follow your direction for my life for you are a God who hears and will not forsake us. Thank you for hearing me today, Father. I love you Lord.*

*In Jesus name I ask these things. Amen.*

Brothers and sisters, that is being prayed over in a powerful way. I was the recipient of so many prayers from so many places by so many people.

I tell people there are three things I would love to do in this life, but they will never happen. I would love to play second base for the St. Louis Cardinals. That will never happen (and never would have). I would love to play tight end for the Dallas Cowboys. That's not going to happen either. But the one thing I would love to do but will never be able to is to shake the hands and hug the necks of everyone who prayed for Alicia and me during my illness.

We received prayers from our church, our community, and other churches in our state, churches in other states, and even from a church in Wales. I continue to meet people who tell me, "Oh, you are Tony Peak. Man, I really prayed for you."

Thank God for his powerful answers to powerful prayers.

***God is great, and I am grateful for faithful prayer warriors!***

# CHAPTER 3

# Merry Christmas!

*The Encouragement of Finding Reasons to Rejoice*

Christmas Day, 2020. My Christmas gift would be having no sedation that day. I wonder if the shepherds in that Judean sheep pasture over 2000 years ago may have thought they were experiencing the hallucinatory effects of sedation too, or if what they were experiencing were the real deal.

I mean, how often does someone receive an angelic message like this? "Fear not: for, behold, I bring you good tidings of great joy, which shall be to all people.

For unto you is born this day in the city of David a Saviour, which is Christ the Lord. And this shall be a sign unto you; Ye shall find the babe wrapped in swaddling clothes, lying in a manger" (Luke 2:10-12 KJV).

And then for an encore, how about a divinely inspired concert? "And suddenly there was with the angel a multitude of the heavenly host praising God, and saying, 'Glory to God in the highest, and on earth peace, good will toward men" (Luke 2:13-14 KJV).

Not Covid, not cancer, not heart disease, nor any other malady known to man can eliminate the Good News delivered by God's angel that night. If you have never experienced the miracle of Christmas along with the miracle of Easter, you are missing out on the best experiences you could have in this life and the life to come. Praise God from whom all blessings flow!

Alicia arrived for a Christmas Day visit to find three gifts left for her by Nurse Andrea. There were three framed blue imprints of my hands Nurse Andrea had prepared for Alicia, our grandchildren, and our church. Nurse Andrea is a Christmas miracle.

For medical and insurance reasons I would soon need to be moved to another facility. Alicia began to weigh the options for moving me to a LTACH, Long-Term Acute Care Hospital. Alicia's journal contains the many notes of information she had gathered from the various hospitals on the radar screen for my transfer.

On Monday, December 28, Alicia was running errands in Shawnee when she received a phone call from Dr. Tony. The quality of my vitals and condition were migrating south for the winter: fever of 105.1, oxygen saturation rate down to 77% (above 90% is optimal), oxygen through ventilation up to 100%, heart rate over 150 beats per minute. My heart had gone from beating to basically vibrating.

For the third time in a series of critical times, doctors called Alicia to the hospital, being told I would not survive. For those anxious moments, Alicia had the support of her good friend, Terri Williams. Also joining Alicia were our two adult-age children, Kaitlyn and Cody. Things grew so tense;

Terri was asked to leave the room and Kaitlyn and Cody never made it into the room.

*Monday, December 28*

"God saved Tony Gene Peak today!"

I had made it another day.

*Wednesday, December 30*

*We met Dr. Gaynell Anderson, a.k.a. Wonderful Physician and Prayer Warrior Extraordinaire. Part of her treatment plan includes praying over her patients.*

She filled Alicia in on my vital signs which were all basically in an acceptable range by then.

That day would also find Alicia making a huge decision about a LTACH site. The best option seemed to be Carrus Hospital in Sherman, Texas. Sherman is a long way from Tecumseh, but relatively close to the home of our daughter Kaitlyn, in Caney, Oklahoma.

One catch. The ambulance ride there would cost between $15,000 to $20,000. Chicken feed to Bill Gates, but a significant price tag for a preacher and his schoolteacher wife.

Our church family stepped in again in a big way. They established an account from donations made by members of our church and our community which would cover the cost of the ambulance ride, or it could be used for any other Covid-related expenses. If Carrus was to be our destination, God proved again to be Jehovah Jireh, the Great Provider.

In my later days of recovery at home, as Alicia and I discussed those times and from the information I gathered from her journal and Facebook logs, I began to have more sympathy for her than I did for myself. While I resided mostly in the La La Land of sedation, Alicia faced the sober reality of anxiety over my health and the decision-making regarding my care.

I believe scripture teaches that God calls the man to be the head of the household. That doesn't mean that the man is the king of the castle, and all the family members are his servants. I'm convinced that being the head of the household means God says to the man, "The buck stops here, buddy. I'm holding you responsible for the direction and condition of your family." That is not much of a fat cat kingship.

I also believe that God has blessed me with a wise and intelligent wife. Our mode of operation in decision making consists of talking out the conditions related to a decision needing to be made. I welcome her input. Then after prayer, I was left to make the final decision. It has been extremely rare during our marriage that the final decision didn't involve Alicia and I being on the same page.

But in those days, Alicia was making the final decisions and without my input. Although that was a new level of responsibility for her by not having me to lean on, it meant she now learned to lean more deeply upon her God.

In this era of an increased popularity of tattoos, maybe it would be helpful for every believer to have Proverbs 3:5-6 tattooed in a conspicuous and easy-access place on the body to be reminded of the deep value that resides within that passage. "Trust in the Lord with all your heart; do not depend on your own understanding. Seek his will in all you do, and he will show you which path to take." (Proverbs 3:

5-6 NLT)

Here is what I've discovered in my time on planet earth. Oftentimes I encounter a heavy problem, and I only see one or two options, and neither of them are very appealing. I even convey that wisdom on to God. But when I trust the solution to Him, He shows me an option that never occurred to me. That is why scripture gives us that "do not depend on your own understanding" part. God gives you a brain and He expects you to use it, but not exclusively. Always give God the first shot at your problem and allow Him to give the final say in its solution.

December 31 would mercifully take us to the precipice of saying goodbye to the year 2020. I mean, who saw that pandemic coming? But it was far from over.

*Thursday, December 31*

*"Tony is working so hard to breathe. His numbers are maintaining. It is so hard to watch him work so hard just to breathe. His eyes are open but mostly just a stare. Every now and then he would blink when I asked a question. His stomach is messed up and the diarrhea is non-stop, so they had to put in a fecal catheter. It will protect the huge bedsore. It killed me to watch him today. I am petrified about what is going to happen in the weeks and months ahead. I keep doing the 'what if's' in life. I am so sad watching him suffer so much. It is heart-wrenching. I just keep praying for God's hand of protection to cover him and give him peace. His eyes just looked so scared. I moved his head, and he grimaced a big grimace, and I pulled a band-aid off, and he did it again. I miss him so much."*

This a place where people usually pull out the clichés; "Life is fragile. Make the most of everyday. Be sure to tell your family and friends how much you love them." But those are clichés filled with heavy meaning. We take so much for granted, especially when life is rocking along smoothly and steadily. But a day that does not contain gratitude to God for his blessings and expressions of love for people is a day wasted. Be a Psalm 118:24 kind of guy or gal. "This is the day the LORD has made; let us rejoice and be glad in it." (NIV)

***God is great and I am grateful for reasons to rejoice!***

# CHAPTER 4

## Happy New Year, Maybe!

*The Encouragement of New Beginnings,
Even If We Don't Understand Them*

Goodbye 2020, hello 2021! New Year's Day found my vital signs in decent shape and the diarrhea stopped. The ventilation assistance came through the CPAP setting which meant I was basically breathing on my own. Respiratory Therapist Kaytie was pumped and kept walking by, looking at my numbers, as if they had been hijacked by monitor gremlins.

I am reminded of a story which I'm told is not true, but still makes a good point. It is the story of a Covid patient who was charged a rather large sum for the use of a ventilator while in the hospital. As he began to cry, the doctor tried to reassure him that everything would be alright. His response was, "I cry not for the bill, but for I have been breathing God's air all my life, but I never paid for it. Now I know how much I owe God."

Oh, how much we owe God! James, the half-brother of

Christ, reminds us in James 1:17, "Every good and perfect gift is from above, coming down from the Father of the heavenly lights, who does not change like shifting shadows," (NIV). Every February 2, the country holds its collective breath to see what the shadow of the ground hog, Punxsutawney Phil, will tell us about the duration of winter. But James tells us the bounty of God's provisions do not change like the shadow of Punxsutawney Phil. Praise God for the very air you breathe!

That inaugural day of 2021 saw Dr. Anderson asking me to move my foot, and I did, ten minutes later. It has happened in cases of patients trying to come out of the fog of Covid and sedation that their responses to commands are often delayed. And if the medical staff is not aware of the delayed responses, some would assume the patient has suffered significant brain damage.

Sometimes a patient just needs the right motivation to respond.

*Saturday, January 2*

*Dr. Anderson stopped by and asked Tony to blink. He wouldn't blink for the doctor, so I said, 'I'll give you a kiss if you blink for Dr. Anderson.' Guess who blinked! He got lots of kisses today!*

*Sunday, January 3,*

*I'm excited to report signs of progress. Tony was exhibiting more body movement, he gave a small head shake when asked, attempted to pucker his lips and to smile, lifted his head and shoulders several times, and he even went to the bathroom on his own.*

Victories come in odd packages sometimes.

Modern medicine sometimes flows through channels of insurance requirements, hospital policies, availability of empty beds, and plain old red tape. In short, I wouldn't be going to Carrus Hospital in Sherman, Texas, but would instead be sent to Select Specialties Hospital in Oklahoma City. This was a huge disappointment to Alicia, but our experience at Select would prove to be a very good one. God works in mysterious ways and even in different cities.

So, on my sixty-seventh birthday, my gift was an ambulance ride to OKC. Switching from the hospital vent to the ambulance vent was a different animal and I responded with heavy, sweat-producing anxiety. (I think God gave me a pass this time on the Philippians 4:6 command to not be anxious about anything).

*Wednesday, January 6*

*God is in control. I am not. Please, Lord, help me be faithful to you and your love for us and to rely on you and what you do for us is best.*

Alicia was able to go with me to the waiting ambulance in Shawnee and bless me with a kiss. She knew that hospital visitation hadn't opened yet at Select, so if she wanted to see me one last time before admission, she would have to be at the hospital as the ambulance arrived. Lucky for us, our dear friend Terri was there to drive Alicia as they followed the ambulance.

Wednesday, January 6 was a very rainy day. The ambulance driver had one goal in mind - to transport Tony to Oklahoma City as quickly as possible. Terri had one goal in mind - to keep up with the ambulance so her good friend, Alicia, would be able to see her husband one last time before being admitted. The ambulance driver's desire to achieve his goal led to speeds of up to 95 miles per hour. Terri's desire to achieve her goal matched the ambulance driver's speed. In pouring rain, our determined friend chased an ambulance at speeds of almost 100 miles per hour westward on Interstate 40 toward Oklahoma City.

I hope and pray that the statute of limitations for a speeding violation has covered Terri's driving that day. After all, "A friend loveth at all times, even to the point of putting the pedal to the metal." Amen.

# SECTION III

# OKLAHOMA CITY LOOKS, OH, SO PRETTY

# CHAPTER 5

# For Better or for Worse

*The Encouragement of a Loving Spouse*

Oklahoma City is the capital and largest city of Oklahoma. The population reached 681,054 in the 2020 census. The city is the eighth-largest in the United States by area including consolidated city-counties. It is in the middle of an active oil field, and oil derricks dot the state capitol grounds. Oklahoma City was founded during the Land Run of 1889 and grew to a population of over 10,000 within hours of its founding.

It is the site of the April 19, 1995, bombing of the Alfred P. Murrah Federal Building, in which 168 people died, the deadliest terror attack in U.S. history until the attacks on the World Trade Towers in New York City on September 11, 2001.

Its beauty is duly noted in the lyrics of the song "Route 66"; "Oklahoma City looks oh so pretty." And this pretty city would be my home away home from January 6, 2021, through April 20 of the same year. And my first home address would be at Select Specialties Hospital, 3524 NW 56th Street, Oklahoma City, Oklahoma, 73112.

Life at Select initially went as expected, Alicia getting acclimated to new policies and procedures, a balancing act with respiration and other vitals, increased attention to my bedsore wound, and developing lines of communication between Alicia and the hospital staff. My case manager, Beth Leonard, would prove very helpful to Alicia in the communication process.

On Saturday, January 9, Charles White, a former member of our church and an all-around great guy, took over my ICU room in Shawnee when I left. That Saturday, he went home to be with Jesus.

This is the big dilemma for the believer in Christ. If you love someone, naturally you want the absolute best for them. And what is better for your loved one than to travel into the arms of the Lord to spend eternity with Him and enjoy all He has in store there? Then, why do we hurt so when we lose a loved one who is a believer? That is because the departure leaves a hole that nothing else can fill.

Think of life as an ongoing jigsaw puzzle. We are the pieces of that puzzle. As people are born, the puzzle begins to expand. And as people die, the pieces of the puzzle representing their lives are removed, leaving painful holes in the lives of those that are left here to grieve for them.

Grieving is a natural part of dealing with the hole. Paul comforts us with the words from 1 Thessalonians 4:13-18 NIV,

> [13]**"Brothers and sisters, we do not want you**

to be uninformed about

those who sleep in death, so that you do not grieve like the rest of

mankind, who have no hope. ¹⁴ For we believe that Jesus died

and rose again, and so we believe that God will bring with Jesus

those who have fallen asleep in him. ¹⁵ According to the Lord's word,

we tell you that we who are still alive, who are left until the coming

of the Lord, will certainly not precede those who have fallen asleep.

¹⁶ For the Lord himself will come down from heaven, with a loud

command, with the voice of the archangel and with the trumpet

call of God, and the dead in Christ will rise first. ¹⁷ After that, we who

are still alive and are left will be caught up together with them in the

clouds to meet the Lord in the air. And so we will be with the

Lord forever. ¹⁸ Therefore encourage one another with these words."

After returning to my ministry at the church in August of 2021, our congregation suffered the loss of a few members whose deaths left holes in the hearts of grieving spouses left behind. Sensitized, I suppose, by knowing what Alicia went through at the prospect of my dying, I looked for ways to comfort them which even included the hopes of bringing back their spouses that had passed. I deeply wanted to refill the holes and renew the loving couples.

Of course, this is not impossible. Our God is a resurrecting God. But a resurrection from the dead is unlikely here on earth. Yet the resurrected would have to face death again someday. But find comfort in this. I believe, should our departed loved ones be given a chance to return after unpacking their luggage in heaven, they would graciously decline. They might respond to us by saying something like, "I love you deeply and I long to be with you, but for me to return to that rock called Earth, no chance. Heaven is my home, and I choose not to roam."

Covid, cancer, heart attacks, traffic accidents, war, and other calamities leave a wake of broken hearts grieving death but take Paul's advice. Go ahead and grieve, but not a hopeless grief; but a hope-filled grief that assures you that the hole in your life is temporary, but life with your loved one again in heaven is eternal. And I researched it. Eternity is a long, long time.

*Monday, January 11, Beth was able to let Alicia FaceTime with me. When I FaceTimed with him, he was very despondent and depressed. He would hardly look at me or make eye contact with me, but he mouthed the words, "I want my wife to take me home.*

Alicia couldn't take me home, at least not at that time. But one day the Lord will take us home where He "will wipe every tear from their eyes. There will be no more death or mourning or crying or pain, for the old order of things has passed away," (Revelation 21:4, NIV). That is about the best news for those looking to fill painful holes in their lives.

Life at Select continued to move at a snail's pace for me (and that is a snail with a limp). Dead skin had appeared on my bedsore wound and plans were being made to remove it. Visitation still wasn't allowed, but I was able to FaceTime with Alicia. I had even progressed to a point where I was able to ask to FaceTime.

My progress led doctors to set February 9 as a target date for my dismissal. Then off to home sweet home. I couldn't wait to be in my own house, sleeping in my own bed, watching birds, squirrels, rabbits, foxes, turkeys and deer coming up to eat in our own backyard. Dorothy from the Wizard of Oz nailed it. "There is no place like home."

Tuesday, January 13, was significant for no other reason that it was Day 50 of being in hospitals. But then came Wednesday.

*Wednesday, January 15*

*His biggest prayer request is for muscle strength and nerve recovery. He still cannot move anything.*

Friday, January 16, hangs in a fog of my memory, but I vaguely remember Nurse Zobia delivering more balloons from well-wishers to my room and read to me several new get-well cards. She asked, "Are you sure you aren't a celebrity?" If this is celebrity, please give me anonymity.

Saturday, January 17

*I asked Tony to move his hands and HE WAS ABLE. He also*

*moved his leg off the bed.*

I was practically Olympics worthy!

Covid-19 claimed another victim on Sunday, January 18. Alicia got word that my pastor friend, Justin Dunn, lost his father that day. I have no love for Covid.

On Wednesday, January 20, Alicia found me entertaining a mood of deep depression. I begged her to come get me and take me home. She tried to calm me by telling me that she would bring me home as soon as possible. My reply stung her, "Don't lie to me." Of course, that did nothing to lift her spirits, yet she was still hopeful.

*Wednesday, January 20*

*His discharge date is now around February 9, 3 weeks from today! I plan on bringing him home to continue to recuperate unless something drastic happens.*

Something drastic happened.

Alicia had been to dinner with the Williams that day. Afterward, she and Terri went to visit Terri's mother. Alicia got a call from Select that and in her words, "all heck broke loose." The nurse making the call told her to get to the hospital ASAP.

The Williams chauffeured Alicia to the hospital and she was allowed to come into my ICU room. There she found a team of ten hospital personnel trying desperately to pull me back from death's door. Two were taking turns "bagging" me (a process in which the person attending inserts the end of the bag in my trachea and began squeezing the bag to ventilate me).

The hopes of dismissal and my recovery bottomed out... again. My heart rate rose extremely high, and my oxygen level dropped extremely low. For the fourth time in our journey, Alicia was told my chances of survival were very slim to none, and mostly none.

For Alicia time stood still. She saw her husband with a face so swollen it looked like it could pop at any moment. I guess I have some elasticity to my skin because she said the swelling got to a point unimaginable.

There would be some agonizing hours for family and friends. Terri and David Williams were with Alicia at the hospital. Alicia called our children, Kaitlyn and Cody, and they both made plans to meet her there. Other family members would arrive to be a part of a night long vigil in the Select waiting room as members of our church and community once again went to their knees in prayer.

A FaceBook post from that day by Danielle Kasaske, a former member of our youth group said, "Everyone STOP what you're doing and PRAY for Pastor Tony Peak! In my eyes he will always be my Youth Pastor, the man who led me to Jesus, and the brother that baptized me." Prayer warriors were at it again.

Although the swelling in my face began to recede, the danger didn't. The hospital staff told Alicia, family, and friends, to say goodbye. Wednesday night bled into Thursday. Family and friends rotated taking shifts at the hospital. Thursday evening, my good friend, Richard Bailey, who is an ordained minister, was allowed into my room to pray for me. Richard has such a compassionate heart, and it is easy for me to visualize him delivering his heart-felt prayer with tear-filled eyes.

Weeks after this I would be told by Alicia that more than once, I had held hands with the Grim Reaper. To hear I almost died multiple times was obviously unsettling, but it never really hit home so hard as when I later read a FaceBook post from Terri Williams from January 21. "With a heavy heart, I want to share an update on Tony. The doctors have told the family the pneumonia has progressed; therefore, the time Tony has left on this earth is hours to days. They would covet your prayers for peace and comfort for him, as well as, for them during his remaining time on earth. The blessings you have shared through your prayer support is immeasurable! Tony would be so proud of his immediate family and his church family for the way they have upheld each other during this difficult time. We love you all and thank you for everything you have done. Please continue to pray as their hearts are breaking."

I believe reading Terri's post hit me like a ton of bricks because in the past I had prayed such prayers for people. I had asked our church members to pray such prayers for people. And those situations had always ended in death.

This is a Facebook post from Kaylie Haddox, the daughter of Tracy Reynolds, a former youth group member. "My heart is so heavy tonight as we prepare to lose a great man. A man that has shown up for my family time and time again. From driving to Illinois for my great grandma's funeral, to driving to OU (Medical Center in Oklahoma City) when I had my (son) Kade. The point is he didn't have to. But he did. My heart is in pieces just thinking about him going to heaven…Please pray for peace and comfort of Alicia and family."

On January 22, Alicia posted a picture of the feet of our son-in-law's girls basketball team in Caney, Oklahoma, huddled in a circle before a game, wearing red bows on their shoelaces, in support of Kaitlyn's dying dad.

Get the picture? These were darkest of dark days in the life of our family and friends. Then God showed up in a miraculous way. Everything about my condition began to show improvement. God is great, and I am grateful. Once again, the Grim Reaper would leave my hospital room disappointed.

Regular visitation opened up at the hospital on Monday, January 25. Alicia would be able to visit me from 2-6 p.m. each day. Let me pause here to quote the question asked in Proverbs 31:10 (NIV). "A wife of noble character who can find?" I don't know about other guys, but I found my wife of noble character and married her on November 19, 1982, at Chisholm Heights Baptist Church in Mustang, Oklahoma.

From the time that visitation was opened at Select until my dismissal from Physicians Hospital in Anadarko on Friday, June 4, 2021, Alicia did not miss a single day of coming to visit me. That included a span of about four days in February 2021 when much of Oklahoma was hit with snow, ice, and sub-freezing temperatures. Never once did she call and say, "I'm really tired tonight. I think I'll go home, and I'll see you tomorrow". When she arrived for visitation it was always with a brave and buoyant smile on her face. Who smiles every single day for 131 days? Alicia Marie Peak, a wife of noble character.

Understand that those days were some really trying and dismal days. The best part of my day was seeing her walk through my hospital room door. The worst part of my day was seeing her walk out. When the nurse would turn off my room lights for the night, I would ask her to leave the light on in the bathroom. That wasn't because I was afraid of the dark. It was that having the light on seemed to make the loneliness more bearable.

Ephesians 5:25 (MSG) gives us our marching orders guys. "Husbands, go all out in your love for your wives, exactly as Christ did for the church—a love marked by giving, not getting." Be intentional about telling your wife how much you love her, then show her how much you love her. Every day. Make a call. Buy a card. Give a gift. Plan a date night. Help with household chores. Take the kids for a night and let her have a night that allows her some "me time."

A wife of noble character. If you have one, love her every day.

And ladies, if you have the love of a good man who treats you like a queen as you so deserve, demonstrate that you love and appreciate him. But let me give you a way of showing love to your husband that is so simple, but so powerful. Men want to know they are doing a good job. With words of affirmation and appreciation you can boost his confidence to the moon to continue to work for you and your family.

You think that isn't important? Dr. Gary Chapman, psychologist and author of *The Five Love Languages* tells of a time when a frustrated wife visited his office complaining she could not get her husband to paint the house. Dr. Chapman asked her if he ever did anything well for her. She conceded that there were things he would do that she appreciated. Dr. Chapman then instructed her to go home and never mention painting the house again, but continually affirm him when he did do kind and helpful things.

Sometime later, the wife returned to Dr. Chapman telling him that she had done as he instructed and in time, without her complaining and prodding, he miraculously began to paint the house.

Ladies, just let your guys know they are doing a good job.

**God is great, and I am grateful for a loving spouse!**

# CHAPTER 6

# Go Ahead, Make My Day

*The Encouragement that Comes from Celebrating Each Day*

On Saturday, January 30, Alicia noticed I was trying to mouth out a message. Inserting the trach tube leaves one unable to speak. So, she leaned in and tried to read my lips to decipher what vital message I had for her. She finally interpreted what I was mouthing. "Super Bowl." I wanted to make sure I could see the Super Bowl. I was on the mend!

Alicia pulled up her Fox Sports app on her phone to show me who was still in the playoffs, and when the Super Bowl would be played. She promised to be sure I got to see it.

An interesting thing happened at this period. This was the time I "woke up." My coherent days would come and go as I was aware enough to recall some of what happened in those days. No more "sedation tribulation." But it turns out the "waking up" was more of a process than a one-day event.

When Alicia and I would later tell people about this waking up period of our journey, she would often say it occurred in very late January or early February. I never said anything about that, but in my mind, I would disagree with her because I remembered being awake for both Super Bowls in 2021. They played two Super Bowls that year because of Covid. I could remember watching the January Super Bowl which was won by the Kansas City Chiefs. In February I watched those same Chiefs be defeated by the Tampa Bay Buccaneers in Super Bowl Two.

If you are any kind of sports fan, you know that didn't happen. But I thought it did, all the way up to the week after Christmas in 2021. I began to question myself. Why would Covid cause the NFL to stage two Super Bowls in one year? Covid was the cause of a multitude of disruptions, but not this one. I got on a sports app and looked up who won the Super Bowls in 2021. The Buccaneers won THE ONLY SUPER BOWL that year. Waking up was definitely a process, not an event.

Another significant take-away from that period was dealing with not being able to speak. When I woke, I was so foggy, I never asked anyone why I couldn't. I just knew I couldn't and mouthing out my communication was my only option. At this point, my arms, hands, and fingers were so weak, I wasn't even able to write out my messages.

Alicia and the poor nurses would try diligently to read my lips. We would all fight our way through those occasions until finally they were able to make out a word or two, and I would be able to convey to them what I wanted them to know. Most nurses would struggle but would eventually get it. There was one nurse who never did get it. Lip reading was not her native language. She would guess and guess at what I was saying yet would never come close. One day we were struggling through the lip reading and she was guessing everything she could think of. I tried one more time, then she said, "You want a taco?" I had a feeding tube in my stomach! What would I do with a taco? The sweet nurse gave up and began bringing another nurse with her to interpret any future lip-reading sessions she and I would have.

But not all was humorous. I am a preacher, and a preacher without a voice isn't of much use. I feared that my preaching days were over and wondered what I would do as a ministry and career when I was released from the hospital. That was a discouraging and depressing prospect.

One day during a visit from Alicia, I got up the nerve to mouth out the words to her, "Is there any chance I will ever be able to talk again?" I'll never forget the overwhelmingly sympathetic look on her face as she exclaimed, "Oh, sweetheart, I'm so sorry. I thought you knew. You can't speak because of your trach tube. When they remove it you will be able to talk again!"

What an absolute relief! There would come a time when I could kiss lip reading goodbye (no pun intended…okay, maybe a little intended) and speak to my heart's content. When the trach tube was removed, I didn't automatically begin speaking again. Some wonderful speech therapists would come to my room several times a week to basically teach me to speak again.

But I now speak. Not like before my illness, but I do speak. One day after I had returned home, Sheila Powell, my home health care physical therapist, asked me, "Has your voice always been that low?" "No, I used to sing tenor in a men's quartet at my church." Those quartet days would be over, but that was okay. I had a voice! I didn't care if my voice sounded like Donald Duck's or Popeye's. I had a voice!

Actually, I've grown fond of the raspy sound of my voice. It has a kind of Clint Eastwood quality to it. Come by my home some day and you can hear me say, "Go ahead, make my day." I'm still working on the Eastwood scowl.

God did make my day and continues to do so. Psalm 118:24 (NKJV) proclaims, "This is the day the LORD has made; We will rejoice and be glad in it."

Psalm 118 is part of what is called the Hallel psalms, reserved for the Jews to sing in days of holidays and celebrations. But what makes a holiday a holiday?

Someone prints it on a calendar? Every day that contains Jesus is a day worth celebrating.

Now in the dark times, you may have to make the choice to rejoice and turn on the party lights in your life, but that is doable, and profitable. If you are having a day that is less than ideal, go to your calendar, and write down something declaring that it is a holiday. It could be "I'm Still Breathing Day" or "I Was Blessed to Have Something to Eat Today Day," "I Have a Job Day." There is always a reason to rejoice for no other reason than a great God created the day.

Go ahead, make your own day!

**God is great, and I am grateful for every blessing He pours into every one of my days!**

# CHAPTER 7

# A Friend that Sticks Closer Than a Brother

*The Encouragement of Friendships*

Saturday afternoon, January 30 brought a big surprise. Alicia woke me and said, "Tony, Lanny Neal is here!" Flash back with me about sixty years to August, 1960. I was on the threshold of launching my public education career in first grade at Cameron Elementary School in Sulphur, Oklahoma. My father dropped off Judy, my older sister, and me at the playground entrance. Judy was a veteran student about to enter the sixth grade. I was a green beginner.

Judy politely, but firmly, informed me that she was heading to the side of the playground designated for the kids of her age. She pointed me in the direction where we little kids were to hang out. There I stood, alone, not seeing a soul I knew. Slowly, apprehensively, I made my way toward the imposing territory of swing sets, jungle gyms, and unfamiliar faces.

On my way, I was approached by a fellow my age sporting a flat top haircut and a huge smile. "Hi, I'm Lanny." I had a friend! Social tragedy was averted. The playground suddenly turned from an enemy to an ally, all because of a kid named Lanny Neal.

Lanny and I would spend part of our time in elementary school years together before he transferred to the other elementary school in town. But in junior high we would reconnect to have six years of solid camaraderie. Time (nor good taste) allows me to recall some of our adventures together. Suffice it to say, Lanny was one of my best buds.

After high school graduation, we drifted to different colleges, and sadly drifted apart. Between our high school graduation in 1972 and this day in Select Specialties Hospital in 2021, we had seen each other only on only a handful of occasions, but the news of my illness and the will of a great God (I refer you again to the book title) brought Lanny to my hospital room in ICU. He was the proverbial sight for sore eyes, along with everything else that was sore on my body.

After a big hello, the next thing out of the mouths of Alicia and I was the question, "How did you get in here?" Hospital visitation had been opened, but it wasn't opened like an Oklahoma land run. Conditions to enter for visitation had to be met, a friendly but firm receptionist in the hospital lobby had to be satisfied, and the proper visitation times had to be observed. At that point, Lanny was 0 for 3.

Lanny answered, "I just walked in a door down there." He would not be a stranger to my room in this hospital and in others to come. Each time he came, Alicia and I wondered how he got in unscathed. I do have a theory. Lanny claims to work for the U.S. Postal Service, but I believe he is employed by another federal government entity, the Central Intelligence Agency. How else could the brother continue to enter hospitals undetected except that he had the skills acquired as an agent for the CIA?

His visits would be medicinal for me, and it brought to mind the sound words of King Solomon in Proverbs 18:24, "A man of many companions may come to ruin, but there is a friend who sticks closer than a brother." I have a brother, Danny, and we have been very close throughout our lives. Danny is not just a brother, but also a good friend; yet Solomon points out the high value of having a brother who has your back but is not of your bloodline.

Contrasting other "friend" verses in Proverbs with 18:24 leads us to understand that there can be two types of friends. There are friends who are in the relationship for what it might profit them, and there are friends who don't care if you have a nickel to your name. We need the latter, and we need to be the latter to our friends.

The story of David and Jonathan rings the bell of what the better kind of friendship should be. Jonathan was the son of King Saul of Israel. David had become a faithful servant of Saul's, but Saul's mental and spiritual shortcomings had rendered David as his enemy in the mind of the king.

Jonathan was the son of royalty, living the life of royalty. He wanted for nothing and had little to gain from befriending this former sheepherder, David. But there was forged a bond between them that would bring Jonathan to be a friend closer than a brother, even closer than a father. Jonathan's faithfulness to his friend would help spare David's life more than once. Ultimately, their friendship wasn't able to continue to protect David from the wrath of the king. Kingly power and hate trumped the togetherness of pals.

The final departure between this exemplary fraternity is described in

1 Samuel 20:42 (NIV), "Jonathan said to David, "Go in peace, for we have sworn friendship with each other in the name of the LORD, saying, `The LORD is witness between you and me, and between your descendants and my descendants forever.' Then David left, and Jonathan went back to the town." I'm sure the two friends parted in tears.

Scripture doesn't record David and Jonathan seeing each other after that day. But their friendship remained true, even past Jonathan's death. When David became king of Israel, one day he asked a servant if there were any descendants from Jonathan's family to whom he might show kindness. There was. Jonathan had a crippled son named Mephibosheth. Mephibosheth is one of the classic names in the Bible. As you say "Mephibosheth," it just flows off the tongue. Alicia loves that name and if she had her way our son, Cody, would have been named Mephibosheth.

I don't know that David loved the boy's name, but he certainly loved the boy's father. 2 Samuel 9:6-7 (NIV) records the first meeting between David and the son of his good friend.

> [6] **"When Mephibosheth son of Jonathan, the son of Saul, came to**
>
> **David, he bowed down to pay him honor.**

> David said, 'Mephibosheth!'
>
> (Notice the joy of David as evidenced by the exclamation point?) 'At
>
> your service,' he replied. ⁷ 'Don't be afraid,' David said to him, "for
>
> I will surely show you kindness for the sake of your father Jonathan.
>
> I will restore to you all the land that belonged to your grandfather
>
> Saul, and you will always eat at my table.'"

And David did just as he promised. This wealthy king of Israel had nothing to gain from a relationship with the young man. Nothing to gain but the blessing of honoring the memory of his tried-and-true friend that stuck by him closer than a brother.

Lean in again, fellows. As you continue to be intentional about earnestly loving the wife of your youth, you still need to develop the love of at least one good friend. Brigette Nichol is credited with this powerful statement, "How beautiful it is to find someone who asks for nothing but your company."

Lanny was that kind of friend. During my illness and recovery, he continued to keep my name before his Sunday School class at Quail Springs Baptist Church in Oklahoma City, asking them to weld the name of his sick buddy squarely in their prayers.

On December 10, 2021, I had the privilege of attending the Christmas party of Lanny's Sunday School class, thanking

Tony Peake

them for their diligent prayers and showing them the fruits of those prayers, as the once paralyzed preacher walked to the podium to share the story of our great God, and my gratitude for what this great God had done for me.

It is worth noting that in those times other friends of mine sent well wishes my way as well. For example, Russell Watson, a former teammate on our high school baseball team, posted on social media that he gave me credit for his happy marriage. Between my freshman and sophomore years at Murray State College in Tishomingo, Oklahoma, I convinced Russell, a recent high school grad, to come down and play catcher for our team at Murray. It was at Murray that Russell met his wife, Edy. I appreciate his kind words and I'm glad he married so well, but I think my main concern was getting the team a good catcher.

I even got a get-well card from Dean Ross, my former baseball coach at Murray State College in Tishomingo, Oklahoma. Best medicine of the day!

Now, guys and gals, I have an assignment for you. Yes, I am a pastor: but before entering the ministry, I was a teacher, so I know something about making assignments. Here it is – if you have a Jonathan in your life (or Jonathanette), be intentional about affirming your appreciation for his or her friendship as soon as possible. Write it down, in your day-timer or in your heart, to set a specific time to do a specific act to acknowledge this specific friend. And if you are fortunate to have a squad of Jonathans or Jonathanettes, do the same for each of your squad members.

Since getting out of the hospital, Lanny and I have made the effort to spend time together, both us and our wives, and just the two of us. Lanny is a guy who appreciates the value of friendships and works to create them and maintain them.

God didn't inspire Solomon to write Proverbs 18:24 just to give the wise old king something to do. God desires for you to have close friendships in which both desire to give and to receive.

Another example of friendship flows into this story courtesy of my friend, Richard Bailey. In the book's introduction I mentioned preparing for a deer hunt in November of 2020 on a piece of Richard's property. Falling ill to Covid that next week, I wasn't able to make the hunt.

A few weeks later, Richard was pheasant hunting on the property where my hunting gear was located. The weather had been wet there recently in Medford, Oklahoma, so Richard had walked in for his hunt, unable to drive his truck all the way up to the property on the mud-mired road. As such, he also wasn't able to drive in and get my hunting gear for me. He made a mental note to come back on a later and drier day to get them.

On his next trip, Richard drove into the field only to find my ground blind, chairs, and corn feeder were missing. I suppose someone in Grant County, Oklahoma, decided he needed my hunting equipment more than I did and had appropriated said equipment.

Richard was none too thrilled with the theft of my property. He ran an ad in the local paper that read as follows.

"$1000 Reward for the information leading to the arrest of whomever stole a corn feeder and deer blind and other miscellaneous items, 2 miles South & ½ mile east of K Electric sign on Highway 11. The items belonged to a Preacher that is in the hospital for 80 days fighting for his life with Covid."

After I was dismissed from the hospital, Richard came to my house to visit and gave me a copy of the ad. Then he added, "They didn't print all of the ad as I gave it to them. At the end of the ad it was supposed to read, "I'd give a thousand dollars to meet the sucker who would steal from a man in the hospital.""

That is a friend.

One final word on friendships. Most teenagers crave friendships. I'm certain the phrase "hanging out" is of adolescent origin. As a youth minster, back in the day, on occasion I would be approached by a member of the youth group distraught over the fact he or she didn't have a close friend, much less a tight posse of friends.

I would offer these young people two-pronged advice. First, to have a friend you must be a friend. This little poem of wisdom says, "I wanted a friend, but I didn't have any. I became a friend, and I had many." The second part of the advice I would offer was, God may not be leading you into friendships now because He wants to build up your friendship with Him.

Yes, God is great (and greatly to be praised), and He is due a huge measure of respect from us, dare I say, even a healthy type of fear of Him; but God also wants to be our friend. There is a friend that sticks closer than a brother, sister, father, mother, spouse, teammate, the dogcatcher, the checkout clerk at Wal-Mart, or any other relationship you might encounter. And that Friend is none other than Jehovah God, the Grand Creator of the Universe.

God placed every star in the sky and knows them by name, yet He also knows the number of hairs on your head (being follicle-challenged [*changed from follicly*], I believe knowing the number of hairs on my head is not that big an accomplishment). You will never have a friend who will stick closer with you than the Lord. Remember our definition earlier of a true friend – one who is a friend not solely for what he or she might receive from the relationship? Extrapolate that definition to Almighty God. What does He have to gain from being our friend? He has everything He needs because He owns everything there is. The only thing God wants from you is your heart; and believe me, if you give Him your heart, it will all be to your good, my friend.

Well, that was a deeper sermon on friendship than I originally intended for it to be. I feel like I should now give an altar call or at least take up an offering! Let's wrap it up like this – be a friend and have a friend, my friends.

***God is great, and I am grateful for faithful friends.***

# CHAPTER 8

## Gonna Make It

*The Encouragement of Staying the Course*

Sunday morning, January 24, brought more frigid temperatures, but an opportunity to FaceTime with Kaitlyn and the grandkids, plus David, Terri, and Shiane Neiman. Shiane is a church member, a sweet young lady, a committed Christian, and my fantastic hair stylist. Just remember, in me, she didn't have much hair to worry over. Nevertheless, she would later travel the fifty miles to give me my first haircut in months.

The next day was as challenging as the previous day had been refreshing. As Alicia arrived, I was in the middle of a panic attack. She surmised several reasons for my discontent, and the nursing staff gave medications for them.

Alicia was spent by the end of that day but was replenished by fajitas brought to her by Terri (more of that good friend stuff).

My fantastic nurses kept up the ongoing challenge of balancing blood pressure, oxygen, and creatine levels. Dr.

Amed came by to adjust my antibiotics and give more Lasix for swelling that was plaguing me in recent days. Dr. Mohammed also stopped in and reassured Alicia that I was in pretty good shape for the shape I was in.

It was along this time that my lungs were introduced to something referred to as "spontaneous breathing." This was a process designed to wean me off the ventilator by giving me opportunities to breathe naturally. It was a positive technique that had negative psychological effects on me. Breathing naturally encouraged the lungs and associated muscles to become stronger in order to one day breathe on their own, but the process also made me feel like I couldn't get enough oxygen and breathing seemed to be a huge struggle.

Tuesday, February 3, Alicia arrived for her daily visit (Hurray!) Since my arms, hands, and fingers weren't strong enough to hold a Bible or book, I asked Alicia to bring me a book by one of my favorite authors, Max Lucado, to read to me each day. My idea was I felt like I had been in the hospital for what seemed the better part of a decade, so surely Brother Max had written a new book or two or ten by now. It would be so good to hear Alicia read the words of one of his new works.

Instead of purchasing a new book, Alicia went to the bookshelf in my office at the church and pulled an old Lucado book off the shelf. Of all the dozens and dozens of books Max Lucado has written and that I own, guess which book she selected? "You Will Get Through This." God has a huge sense of humor leading Alicia to select that book, and I would receive a huge but challenging message from it.

Being a book I already owned, of course, it was one I had already read – in much healthier and happier days. Max's message to hang in there in tough times and there is a God who loves you and will pull you through was one I fully embraced at my first reading. "Thatta boy, Max. That's right, we have nothing to worry about. God is good and He will take care of us." My confidence almost bordered on cockiness. "I can handle anything this world can throw at me," I thought. But I didn't know the world would develop a curve ball called Covid that did its best to strike me out. And that changed everything.

Listen, please, to the primary message of "You Will Get Through This" in Max's own words. "You'll get through this. It won't be painless. It won't be quick. But God will use this mess for good. Don't be foolish or naïve. But don't despair either. With God's help you will get through this." (You'll Get Through This, Max Lucado, Chapter 1, p. 3, Thomas Nelson 2013)

Still agreeing with that message in my heart, I now questioned the message in my head. During this waking up period, Alicia began to explain to me what I had been through since November 2020, and what would need to happen for me to go home. Hearing the goals of that "to-do" list, it seemed to me to be about as doable as taking a leisurely stroll to the planet Mars. And this was for a guy who couldn't walk at the moment.

In my mind I had conceded that I would spend the rest of my life in hospitals and nursing homes. That was the fate of others in this world. Why should I think I could escape a similar one?

But Alicia continued to read to me, and I continued to process what she read. Okay, maybe I would get through this, but it wasn't going to happen tomorrow or the next day or even a week from now. My only healthy recourse was to embrace the mantra, "One day at a time." I would begin to try each day to do what the staff asked me to do. I didn't work for my church now. My occupation was Covid patient recovery. I clocked in each morning when my nurse would come take my vital signs. I would labor throughout the day doing what the doctors, nurses, and physical therapists asked of me. I would clock out at bedtime each day and hope for some restful sleep.

What Max told me, and what God wants to tell you through Max is that success, recovery, victory, and delivery is often involved in that ingredient called patience.

God delivered Daniel from the jaws of the lions, but first Daniel had to spend a night with his furry, feline foes. God would deliver Jacob from his life-long habit of dealing with life through lies and deception, but Jacob would first have to endure the biggest wrestling match of the Old Testament as he grappled with God for an entire night. Paul would be relieved of the torture of the thorn in his flesh, but not until he reached his home in heaven.

Time is a creature with which you have to make peace. Are you currently lying in "the hospital bed" of your own dilemma? The bills just won't get paid, the kids just won't behave, the boss just won't listen, the doctor just can't immediately fix it?

May I suggest you begin your peace talks with time at the peace table of Philippians 4. Verse six instructs, "do not be anxious about anything." Paul, the author of Philippians, defines for you exactly what you are free to worry about – not anything. Well, that certainly narrows down the list, doesn't it?

Maybe you don't worry about the morning paper being delivered late to your doorstep, but you are determined to worry about the difficulties in your marriage.

You won't worry over a traffic light that seems to be permanently stuck on red, but you darn well will worry about the security of your job, the challenges of graduate school, the fate of your family, or the declining health of your body.

What you are saying is that there are some challenges in life that absolutely defy Philippians 4:6. If so, you must be saying that God doesn't know what He is talking about here. Now, let me not be too rough on you. Your struggles may be real, rowdy, and unrelenting. The world is already piling on and you don't need me jumping on the pile too. But grab hold of this, there is assurance that you don't need to worry. Take a peek back in Philippians 4:5. What are the last four words of verse 5? "The Lord is near" (NIV). There is your one-way ticket out of Worryville. The Lord is near. He is so near He hears your heart, He feels your pain, He handles your doubt.

Yes, some of life's challenges drive you to the brink of despair, but not to a place you are called on to be anxious. Your physical or emotional pain may be beyond brutal. Therefore, handling the severity of some of life's biggest beastly challenges requires a monumental amount of faith. Even in that faith, you will still be hammered by the horror of your trial, yet God stands near you assuring you to be anxious for nothing. Anxiety only makes the matter worse.

Allow me a personal example. During the four most critical times in my life when I almost lost my life, I was so out of it that I wasn't aware of my dire circumstances. That meant I couldn't or didn't worry about my life, and God seemed to handle those crises just fine without the benefit of my worrying.

Personally, I can spend too much time developing my relationship with the twins, Familiarity and Comfort. Where you find one, you usually will find the other. As a result, I neglect building relationships with Challenge, Growth, Faith, and Opportunity. And a relationship I'm working to break off is the one with Anxiety. We just aren't compatible. Call it "emotional distancing."

At some point in your life you have to come to a place where you draw a line in the sand and take God at His Word. You may not understand it, but you will embrace it. Now remember we prefaced all this by stating the need to make peace with time. Patience is a virtue. Make patience your partner, not your pain.

"So what do I do while I wait for time to run its course through my situation?"

So glad you asked. Jump from Philippians 4:5 to the last part of 4:6. "... in every situation, by prayer and petition, with thanksgiving, present your requests to God, (NIV).

As you wait, pray, lifting your requests to the Lord who is near. And while you are in your prayer closet, don't forget to give Him your heartfelt thanks. Giving thanks for what God has done for you acknowledges His benevolence towards you.

Ask yourself this question. "Why should I exchange the security of assurance for the uncertainty of anxiety?" Don't be anxious for a single thing.

You will get through this. For 193 days Alicia and I journeyed through hospitals on the way to getting through this; and although I'm light years away from where my health was, we are still journeying to get through this. We are and we will.

One night after I arrived home, I was lying in the hospital bed we had rented and placed in our living room, and I was wide awake. Like 4:00 a.m. awake. With nothing much to do, I began to make a list in my mind of things that I had endured during my illness and recovery that, by the grace of God, I no longer had to endure. The list contained items from the highly annoying to the down-right excruciating. Later I logged all of them on my computer. At last count the list was up to 47 entries. Why would I go to the trouble to log those things I had endured? Because I am so grateful for what a great God did for me, I never want to forget it.

Try this. Build your own list. Raise your own Ebeneezer. 1 Samuel 7:12

(NKJV), tells us, "Then Samuel took a stone and set it up between Mizpah and Shen, and called its name Ebenezer, saying, 'Thus far the Lord has helped us.'"

The word, Ebeneezer, means "stone of help". Samuel erected the stone monument to God to remember God's grace and delivery of His people.

Somehow, whether an entry in a journal, a picture of an

important event, or by any other means, lay a stone of remembrance of what God has done for you.

Refer to it from time to time to remind you of how God has worked on your behalf in your past, and believe that He is totally capable of working on your behalf again.

***God is great, and I am grateful for the benefits of patience and faith!***

# CHAPTER 9

# Major Pain

*The Encouragement of Pain*

The month of February turned into a battle involving adjusting heart rate, developing my spontaneous breathing, and enduring the heavy discomfort of my bed sore wound pain. The collar I wore around my neck to hold the dressing over the opening where the trach tube was inserted became a major pain. Trying to breathe was difficult enough without dealing with the feeling I was being strangled by the collar. But the collar was on correctly and could not be loosened any more. At one point I heard Lisa, my respiratory therapist, tell Alicia the collar couldn't be loosened more. Under the dressing she could see clear to my trachea.

Allow me a personal moment to address Lisa should she be reading this. When I was dismissed from Select Specialties Hospital in March 2021, Lisa was kind enough to come to my room and say goodbye. I told her, "I've never both hated and loved a woman as much as I have you." I know I gave her fits, but only because everything in my world was giving me fits. Lisa was doing her job, and if she hadn't, I wouldn't have been able to recover my breathing to the point it is today. God bless you, Lisa, for doing what was best for me despite my protests.

Monotony became my new roommate. Overall, I was making progress, but the progress could only be measured in millimeters. I've seen a giant sloth move faster than my progress rate. But that was my life for now. You get what you get, and you don't throw a fit.

*Sunday, February 7*

*All numbers look good. He is super tired because he is getting days and nights mixed up! I tried a new approach today. I play a song and he moves certain body parts as much as he can during that song. We started with "Amazing Grace" and his hands. Then a new hymn and shoulders, head, tummy, and then legs!! He did do well. You could barely see his legs move but he is attempting everything I asked. Thank you everyone for prayers.*

Here let's introduce a rather sore subject, my sore bottom. I was still entertaining a nasty bed sore wound which was battling to get worse.

*Monday, February 1*

*It was heartbreaking it was to see him in so much pain as the staff cleaned his wound. At one point, Tony actually had two wounds, one just left of center and one just right of center. The two eventually morphed into one. At one time the wound was the diameter and depth of her fist. Life became a constant chore of trying to be repositioned in bed to alleviate the pain.*

Thankfully, I had to rely on the good nurses to continually come in throughout the day and night to reposition me to find a less painful position because I didn't have the strength to roll over in bed myself. They would pack and stuff multiple pillows around my bottom and back trying to find a position for pain relief.

The pain in my bottom had become a huge pain in my side. It hurt like the dickens and I'm told the dickens has a very high threshold for pain. So if a dickens hurts, the pain must be big time. And mine was big time.

This big-time pain was a blessing in a camouflaged costume. Contrast the pain with a condition called congenital insensitivity to pain and anhydrosis (CIPA). It is a rare hereditary disease. It causes those affected by it to be unable to feel pain. At first glance we might think, "No feeling of pain? Bring on the CIPA!" But CIPA can be more of a curse than a blessing.

Pain is one of the warning systems of the body that something is out of whack. You feel pain, you look for the source. You find the source; you look for a solution.

My Uncle Orel Peak was injured when thrown from a horse resulting in paralysis from about the sternum down to the tips of his toes. He was a man of strong constitution and with the help of Aunt Barbara, he went on to forge a highly productive life.

But on one occasion in the hospital he was being transferred from a gurney to a bed when one of his toes became stuck on the gurney. As he continued to be lifted to the bed his toe was broken and came near to being torn off his foot.

Because of Uncle Orel's paralysis he couldn't feel the pain from what was going on. Fortunately, Aunt Barbara was with him and saw what was happening and stopped even further damage. Pain can be valuable.

When in pain, who wouldn't pray "Lord, please take away my pain!" But on occasion, God uses our pain in crazy ways that are for our good.

Your physical pain, as well as your emotional pain can be extreme, but does it have a hidden purpose? Is there some extreme good that can come from extreme bad?

C.S. Lewis has an interesting position on pain. "God whispers to us in our pleasures, speaks in our conscience, but shouts in our pains."

I've never been a big fan of pain. I would avoid it like the plague (which I'm told was pretty painful). As a result, I believe I was sensitive to the pain of others. If I didn't like pain, why should someone else find pleasure in it? If there was anything I could do to help alleviate someone's pain, I was onboard. But after suffering the weeks of constant bedsore pain, my sensitivity to other's pain accelerated like a teenager in a hot rod on a Saturday night.

A few months ago, Alicia received a phone call from Jo Roberts, a woman whose husband, Jeff, was in the hospital battling Covid much like I did. A mutual friend had put her in touch with Alicia, and through the call, Alicia was able to share with Jo what she had learned from her experiences.

We kept up with the couple through Jo's FaceBook posts. Through many of her posts I saw myself from weeks gone by. I, like many, was praying and rooting for Jeff to beat Covid. I knew what he would have to go through to get his victory, a painful and long haul of recovery, but I believed he could make it.

Then came Jo's post on April 19, 2022. "Update on my Jeffy. It grieves me to tell you that Jeffy left this earthly world to be with our Heavenly Father at 6:55 this morning. I know he is so much better now. He is healed as God promised".

That is a hall of fame example of faith through pain.

The late, great pastor and author, Adrian Rogers, told us, "A faith that hasn't been tested can›t be trusted." Pain is a major faith tester. Through Jo's faith, she is, day by day, passing the test of her faith in God. And I believe her faith will pass with flying colors.

My pain for Jo was through the roof when I heard of Jeff's death. I have not a clue of how deep was and is her pain. But as Frank Perretti so eloquently put it in his book, "The Wounded Spirit," "God does not waste an ounce of our pain or a drop of our tears; suffering doesn't come our way for no reason, and He seems efficient at using what we endure to mold character. If we are malleable, He takes our bumps and bruises and shapes them into something beautiful."

There is only one place in this universe where we will be pain free, and this earth ain't it. Heaven awaits those of strong faith who battle through this world's pain.

Whatever pain you are enduring, endure it through a faith in the God who loves you so much He endured the pain of giving His Son into the bowels of physical and spiritual torture just so that one day you might be pain free.

Enjoy pain? Forget it. Overcome pain. You got it.

**God is great, and I am grateful for His provisions through our pain!**

# CHAPTER 10

## Beauty for Ashes

*The Value of Trusting God*

[1] The Spirit of the Sovereign Lord is on me, because the Lord has anointed me to proclaim good news to the poor. He has sent me to bind up the broken-hearted, to proclaim freedom for the captives and release from darkness for the prisoners, [2] to proclaim the year of the Lord's favor and the day of vengeance of our God, to comfort all who mourn, [3] and provide for those who grieve in Zion – to bestow on them a crown of beauty instead of ashes, the oil of joy instead of mourning, and a garment of praise instead of a spirit of despair. They will be called oaks of righteousness, a planting of the Lord for the display of his splendor. *Isaiah 61:1-3 NIV*

It was along this time in early February that I had an eye-opening experience. A commercial came on the television promoting the product as being a great Valentine's Day gift. I immediately thought, "Wait a minute!" When Alicia arrived for visitation that afternoon, I grilled her good.

"Have we had Thanksgiving Day?"

"Yes, we have."

"Have we had Christmas Day?"

"Yes, we have."

"And have we had my birthday (January 6)?"

"Yep, had that too."

I then realized I had missed three of the most important dates on anyone's personal calendar. I felt like aliens had captured me over that period and only returned me to earth after I had missed all the holiday fun.

You must understand that I am like the father on the movie, *Christmas Story* who is described as being "a turkey junkie." I love turkey and I'm only able to feast on it a few times each year. Some complain they don't like turkey because it is too dry. Well, they've never tasted Alicia's turkey. It is so juicy you have to wear a little bucket below your chin to catch the dripping moisture. Her secret is she baptizes the turkey in a brine solution for 2-3 days. The night before Thanksgiving, she stuffs the turkey with apples and puts it in the oven to slowly bake. The next day, she checks the turkey until the telltale red temperature button pops out on its chest. Then it's game on!

I get to carve the turkey, not because I am necessarily good at it, but because I get to sample the delicious meat as I carve. When our dog, Champ the Beagle, was alive, he loved carving time too because I tossed him samples.

Also, I missed out, not just on Christmas Day, but the whole Christmas season!

No fudge, sugar cookies, peanut brittle or peanut butter balls. No myriad of Christmas parties. No singing of Christmas carols. No tree, fellowship with family or exchanging of gifts. As a matter of fact, there was no laborious Christmas shopping in overcrowded stores (Okay, it wasn't all bad).

And my birthday. In 2021, I was given a special pocketknife by good friend and church member, Lee Tate. It would be the only birthday present I would get that year besides the ambulance trip from Shawnee to Oklahoma City.

Here's the deal. Although I hated that I had missed that whole season of my life, that didn't change the grandness of the season. As Americans we still celebrate God's provision for a group of hardy pioneer travelers who escaped the bonds of religious tyranny to worship the Lord in the way they felt led by scripture to do. It didn't change that a king, the King, was born to a virgin in the most unlikely of places, "Bethlehem Ephratha, the least of the clans" (Micah 5:2). It didn't change that the infant King would rise to set free the captives of sin. It didn't change that although I missed my birthday, I still could cling to the richness of being born again and experiencing "there is now no condemnation for those in Christ Jesus" (Romans 8:1 NIV). The worst that Covid could throw at me did not change one iota the fact that we have a great God, and I'm so grateful He gave us the very life of His beloved Son that we might spend an eternity of bliss with Him in heaven.

Valentine's Day came and went with Alicia bringing me a

card and reading it to me. I wasn't able give her anything, but that was characteristic of the times. She gave, and I received.

A perfect storm of winter weather hit Oklahoma soon after that with temperatures never rising above freezing. On February 15 the statewide average temperature was -7 below zero. And snow was everywhere. Now, I'm a snow guy. I love to watch the sky drop its white fluffy stuff. Until recent years, I went snow skiing in Colorado whenever I got a chance. As a kid, snow days meant rabbit hunting days combining the beauty of God's glorious white blanket upon the earth and the possibility of having rabbit for supper. But I missed all that. I was in the ICU at Select and those rooms have no windows. So I missed even gazing at the beautiful white snow.

Alicia and Lanny came to visit bearing frozen cheeks as red as any rose that ever bloomed. Although I missed seeing the snow, I decided I didn't miss the frigid temps.

This was the season when Alicia was staying in a hotel near the hospital in order to have a better chance to get to the hospital. But the snow piled up so much that it became difficult for her to just get out of the hotel parking lot. One day she was rescued by Terri's nephew, Seth, and his four-wheel drive truck. Another day, our case manager, Beth Leonard, came to the motel and picked up Alicia. Now who does that? Well, Beth for one.

One blessing we received was that although this was pipe-bursting weather, we would dodge that bullet. Alicia had stayed in a motel near the hospital in order to make it to visit each day. But when she returned home a few days later, we both feared she would find the floor of our home looking like a kiddy wading pool. God was gracious and all was well and dry at the Peak house!

Blessings often come in gift boxes of disappointment. Now, call me ignorant at this point because that's what I was. I had been blessed throughout my life to have spent very little time in a hospital. As such, I was ignorant of the fact that a hospital room has a call button for the patient to push in order to get the help of a nurse to come to the room. (Yeah, I know. Ignorant.) I relied on catching my nurse coming by the plate glass window of my ICU room and trying to wave her down. My arms were too weak to completely raise them, so I had to try to signal the nurse with "alligator arms," not being able to raise them above my elbows. I also still had no voice, so screaming out for help wasn't an option. So, I asked Alicia if she would bring me a flashlight that I could wave at the nurse as she went by as sort of a distress signal. As a kid, my father, a veteran of the U.S. Navy, had taught me the signal for SOS; but because I had forgotten it, I planned to just wave the flashlight like crazy in hopes of getting help.

Alicia did bring me a flashlight, and I did try to use it that night as a distress signal. And the flashlight didn't work. The next day, Alicia and Nurse Mondai figured out the bulb was no good. Also Nurse Mondai figured out I didn't have a working call button and she got me fixed up with one. I felt I now held the power of the universe in the palm of my hand, all because my flashlight bulb was no good.

In Genesis, the Bible records the story of Joseph, a guy whose bulb was continually burning out. He was left in the dark when his jealous brothers sold him into slavery and told their father that a wild animal had mauled him to death. He was left in the dark when he rose in position in Egypt to become the Numero Uno servant of the powerful Potiphar only to be imprisoned because he shunned the come-on from Potiphar's wife. He was left in the dark when he interpreted the dreams of two cellmates and asked the cupbearer, who was set free, to put in a good word for him with Pharaoh, only to be forgotten. But Joseph was handed a call button when he was eventually released from prison and rose in position to become the Secretary of Agriculture of Egypt and was given the authority to call all the shots for crop production and storage. He used the button to deal with his brothers who came to Egypt in search of food because of the deathly drought in their home region.

Remember, Joseph's brothers didn't recognize him (mascara and hair bangs on a guy can do that). He played some mind games with his brothers until he finally revealed his identity. The big reveal is recorded in Genesis 50:20 (NLT). "You intended to harm me, but God intended it all for good. He brought me to this position so I could save the lives of many people."

"You intended to harm me (burned out bulb), but God intended it all for good (call button)."

When you receive a gift in life neatly wrapped in disappointment and despair, don't be too quick to take the gift to the return counter. Allow God to help you unwrap it and discover your own version of a nurse's call button.

Two old friends met who hadn't seen each other for some time and begin to visit. After a while one friend commented, "You have changed a lot."

The friend replied, "No, a lot has changed me." A lot has changed me. I wouldn't wish what Alicia and I have gone through on my worst enemy, but what Covid meant for harm, God has used for good. I've discovered things about myself. For instance, a guy grows up wanting to know if he is "tough enough" - tough enough to be the man he hopes to be. That's why we play football, adventure out clinging to a lofty tree swing and drop from it into the lake, drive motorcycles, ride bucking bulls, and on and on. Ladies, I know it's crazy stuff, but whoever accused men of being sane?

In my case, I discovered I was a lot tougher than I thought. As a matter of fact, my good friend, Richard Bailey, visited me after I was released from the hospital and told me, "Friend, you are tougher than boot leather."

Now don't think for a moment that I believe my toughness came solely from me.

Psalm 28:7 (NKJV) reveals the source of my toughness. "The Lord is my strength and my shield." But without the countless number of calamities I faced, I never would have known how tough God could lead me to be.

When I felt the Lord calling me to write this book, it didn't come to me as a command to go off in a corner with a laptop and not come out until I had written a book. He has been with me all the way (which includes the time I accidentally erased four chapters when I saved another document to my manuscript file!).

With God, writing this book has been a strong collaboration on a tough assignment.

Many people are tougher than they imagine, but they won't

realize it until they face their toughest foes. God is beyond tough and waits to be your partner. The caveat to this relationship is God must be your Senior Partner.

Just trust the Lord and keep trying. Let God be the Senior Partner of your toughness team. And thank God for burned out bulbs.

**God is great and I am grateful he makes beauty out of ashes.**

# CHAPTER 11

## Looking Good!

*The Encouragement of True Beauty*

We had two significant events that occurred on Friday, February 19. Lanny got busted and couldn't get through security. Even the best are allowed to have off days.

Of a greater consequence was that Dr. Mohamed was able to balance out my precedex meds. Evidently this was a vital part of being able to move upstairs to a regular room with a window!

I had some fantastic doctors at Select, but Dr. Mohamed was special in that he was not only an excellent physician, but he could also bring sunshine into the cloudiest hospital room. I wish you could hear his high-pitched voice and high volume level with which he would greet me when he would burst into my room on rounds. "Tony, you are looking so good today!" I had no idea how I was looking. I wouldn't see a mirror for six months. But to hear Dr. Mohamed, one would have thought I resembled Hercules. He never stayed long, but it was always long enough to brighten my day.

Sunday, February 21, brought a new level of low. I was sitting up in my bed during the night. My night nurse had just left the room when I opened my mouth and projectile vomited all over my chest. At first, I dealt with the uncomfortable experience of having warm stomach contents all over the front of my hospital gown. As I waited for the nurse to return, the warmth turned cold, and I began to chill.

Over the next few nights I would repeat this process, but we managed to have one of those blue puke bags always at hand. Whoever thought having a puke bag at the ready would be such a huge blessing? (For me and the nurse.)

My nurse was able to convey all this to one of my doctors. They determined the nausea was caused by my intolerance of the formula going through my peg tube into my stomach. Gratefully, the formula was changed, but that would become a process repeated periodically over the next few months to continue to fight off nausea.

Tuesday, February 23, Alicia brought sweet treat cookies from Debra Fletcher to the nurses. I wonder if that had anything to do with the super-duper treatment, I received that day.

Friday, February 26, was a high-water mark. I had progressed to the point of being graduated to the second floor, Room 211! I had a window! I couldn't see much but treetops and blue sky, but that was enough to create a thrill in my soul.

It was then that Alicia decided it was time to personalize my room. She attacked one wall with pictures of us, kids and grandkids; pictures the grands had colored for me; and an onslaught of cards sent almost daily, mostly from some wonderful church members.

But the picture Alicia posted that drew the most attention from my nurses was a copy of a picture from my senior yearbook. It featured me sitting on a stool wearing nothing but a pair of those hideous basketball uniform trunks they made us wear back in the day. Why did we never notice how obscene they were? Thank God for the Fab Five Michigan Wolverines basketball team of 1989 who introduced the world to knee length trunks! My nurses would marvel at all the postings Alicia had made, then ask "Who is that?" Sheepishly, I answered, "That's me."

Let me fast forward and explain the significance of that photo. After I transferred to Physicians Hospital in Anadarko, Oklahoma, I was visited by Physical Therapist Justin. He was there to evaluate my condition and determine the best course of treatment for me. For the first thirty minutes we talked sports – high school, college, and pros. I made bonus points with him when he asked me the trivia question, "What is the name of the mascot of Atoka High School?" With confidence and pride I answered, "The Wampus Cats!" Justin was duly impressed. (I have no idea what a wampus cat is, but I know you can find them in Atoka, Oklahoma.)

He then began the assessment. He first took a look at my lower legs dangling beneath the hem of my hospital gown and said, "Man, those are some emaciated legs!" And he was right.

Now here is the connection of the leggy picture on the wall of my room at Select and Justin's evaluation. Yours truly was the 1972 Sulphur High School Prettiest Legs Contest

Champion! At one time in history my legs were a national treasure; it is actually documented in the 1972 yearbook with the aforementioned photo. Now my legs were nothing but wrinkled skin and shin bones. My skin was so bad that one day I bent down to pull up my wrinkled socks and discovered I wasn't wearing any socks!

Psalm 31:30 informs us that, "Charm is deceptive, and beauty does not last." Yes, we should pay attention to our physical health and display a neat appearance, but we don't live our lives in a way so we can stand in front of the full-length mirror each day and admire our bodies.

Some of the most beautiful people I have known in my life would never pass Hollywood's standard for physical attractiveness. Those folks' beauty doesn't end at their skin, but rather begins under their skin.

I'm not saying folks with good looks are all shallow and conceited. In Genesis 12:11 (ESV), Abram describes his wife, Sarai, as "a woman beautiful in appearance". Genesis 29:17 (ESV) says, "Rachel had a lovely figure and was beautiful." Second Samuel 14:27 (NIV) tells us that Tamar "was a beautiful woman."

Maybe she got her good looks from her father, David, who is introduced in 1 Samuel 16:18 (NASB) as, "a valiant mighty man, a warrior, skillful in speech, and a handsome man;" That verse also says, "and the LORD was with him." Being beautiful or handsome doesn't mean a person is eliminated from service to God.

On the other hand, some are physically unattractive to the point my father used to describe one of these as being "so ugly that he had to sneak up on a dipper to get a drink of water (referring to the old method of getting a drink of well water with a dipper from the well bucket). But all of God's children are beautiful in His eyes. And at the end of the day (and in the beginning), who do you want to see you as beautiful more than God?

David gets a rave review in 1 Samuel 16:18. But he still didn't seem to measure up to his older brothers whom David's father, Jesse, first introduced to the prophet, Samuel, as potential candidates to take over the throne of Israel from King Saul.

As a matter of fact, God warns Samuel not to get caught up in physical attractions. 1 Samuel 16:7 records, "But the LORD said to Samuel, 'Do not look on his appearance or on the height of his stature, because I have rejected him (older brother). For the LORD sees not as man sees; man looks on the outward appearance, but the LORD looks on the heart.'" (ESV)

In the prophecy of the coming Messiah in Isaiah 5:32 (NIV), Jesus is described as having "nothing in his appearance that we should desire him."

I once taught anatomy in high school and, as best as I remember from those days, the heart is an internal feature, even if the word "heart" is used figuratively instead of literally. Can we throw physical appearance out the window when it comes to the character and value of a person? The world doesn't always get it right, but I applaud the fashion industry for using "plus size" models in their ads and commercials today. I mean isn't "plus" considered a plus?

I also applaud those of you who strive to think as God thinks and refuse to look at someone on "appearance or on the height of his stature" (unless you are an NBA scout, then height may be a big deal). And I applaud those parents, teachers, youth workers and any other adult who makes a point to encourage young people to not buy the lie displayed in fashion magazines. Surviving adolescence is brutal enough without weighing down our kids with impossible "Barbie and Ken" expectations for how they should look.

Today my legs have rebounded to the point I can walk without any aid except the help of AFO braces (ankle foot orthosis, used primarily for those suffering from "drop foot"). Actually I can walk barefooted without them, but my gait makes my grandson, Johnny, ask "Why do you walk like that?" Physical Therapist Tori at Anadarko described my shoeless walking style as being like "a baby deer in tall grass."

The point is the prettiest legs won't get you into heaven and the ugliest legs won't keep you out. The most important part is the condition of your heart and if it belongs to the Lord.

**God is great, and I am grateful He looks at our hearts.**

# CHAPTER 12

# Large and in Charge

*The Encouragement of Submitting to God's Sovereignty*

Late February and early March were just days of grinding it out. The bedsore was becoming more sore each day that I was in my bed. Dr. Ahmed continued the slow march toward lowering the vent levels until one day taking me completely off of it. The first of several discussions began with Alicia and the staff concerning what facility I might go to for rehab.

Wednesday, March 3, was the century mark – 100 days in the hospital.

March 9 was a special day of sorts. It hadn't dawned on me, but I hadn't been outside, except to be transferred by ambulance between hospitals, since November 2020. My physical therapist Lisa wanted to get me outside and enjoy some fresh air. Because the weather forecast was calling for nice temperatures for that time of year, I was transferred from my hospital bed into a wheelchair for the first time. My PT would consist of providing my own horsepower to wheel the chair. Except my horse was more along the horsepower of a Shetland. It was a struggle, but I went farther than I expected before I had to be assisted the rest of the way outside.

It was glorious to be outside again, but it was also frigid. The temperature was relatively mild for March in Oklahoma, but it was far from balmy, and I was dressed only in my hospital gown. The hospital gown is highly functional for a patient in a bed, allowing quick access for hospital staff to every body part, but is also very well ventilated. I was cold. The field trip was cut short, and I felt terrible for ruining what Lisa had hoped would be a special treat for me.

On Thursday March 11, they tried to downsize my trach tube, but adhesions caused a lack of sufficient airflow. Eventually they were able to proceed.

*Monday, March 14, 2021:*

*On the funny side I just had the most absolutely embarrassing moment I've had in quite some time. I walked into an unlocked bathroom stall and a woman was sitting on the toilet!!! Apparently when I pushed the UNLOCKED door open, it hit her knees, and she said, 'Ohhhhh, I'm sorry. I should have locked that.' 'You think so?' I was so scared to death, and in a hurry to get out of there, I fell down on top of her. My chest was in her face, all the while trying to push off the back of the wall of the stall and get out of there!!! She thought it was totally funny and just kept giggling!!!*

*Tuesday, March 15*

*He is practicing with a speaking valve and the speech therapist, 15 to 20 minutes a day. He was able to say, "I love you!"*

Finally, on Wednesday, March 17, they capped my trach! The Peak family made their way to America from Ireland many years ago, so maybe it was St. Patrick and the luck of the Irish that brought this good fortune. But the smart money says it was a work of God.

When the trach tube was capped and I was breathing on my own, I began receiving a respiratory command from the doctor and nurses. "Smell the flower, blow out the candle." Translated, that meant no more straight mouth breathing. I was to inhale through my nose (smell the flower) and exhale through my mouth, blowing downward (blow out the candle). I would have that command repeated to me so often that if I could have had a dollar for each time I heard it, I could have paid off half the national debt. But it was all for my benefit.

Friday, March 19, I was given three entire ice chips! It is amazing what tiny things bring such large joy. Dr. Ahmed came by and decided if I had a good weekend, they would completely remove the trach tube on Monday. Monday brought just that. They conducted a barium test in which I had to swallow the barium and let them track it through my system. I passed the test, and I didn't even study! The next step would be to slowly introduce liquids and then foods.

On Thursday, March 25, Alicia got word about me being transferred to a facility in Oklahoma City for rehab. The bad news was I would have to quarantine for two weeks once I arrived there, and then Alicia could only visit twice a week for thirty-minute periods. But my spirits rebounded some when I was allowed some applesauce and thickened cola. It tasted almost as good as a Thanksgiving turkey. Almost, but not quite.

Another big win when was PT Lisa and her crew were able to lift me out of bed with a sling apparatus, and I actually took a few baby steps! Baby steps seemed to be our mode of operation from Day One, so this was no different; but take enough baby steps and you get a happy, mobile baby!

Friday, March 26, became the bearer of bad news. The rehab facility in Oklahoma City denied me because of the severity of my bed sore wound. Another facility in the metroplex area denied me for the same reason. Alicia and Terri continued to visit other facilities hoping to find a good fit.

How about a little good news? Dr. Mohammed stopped in and proclaimed me the Miracle Man of Select Hospital! He told us that at the time I came to Select, the hospital was losing about a patient a day to Covid. The hospital became a dismal place to come to work. So God's miracle not only blessed me, but also blessed a diligent but disillusioned hospital staff.

This would not be the only time I was referred to as the Miracle Man. That thrilled me because people could see I was still alive by the grace of a most gracious God. But I hoped no one would think I thought there was anything special about me that that I would deserve such a miracle.

I've known me, oh, pretty much all my life, and I knew there was and is nothing special about me, in and of myself. I'm just a guy who grew up on a small farm, Route 2, Sulphur, Oklahoma. I am a sinner, saved by grace. The miracles I received were totally a decision made by God.

Which brings up an issue concerning people receiving hope through God's miraculous story in my life. As you read this, you may be thinking of critically ill family or friends whom you faithfully lifted up in prayer for God's deliverance, His answer did not result in them being healed. Let's walk through this together.

I have been asked if I ever asked God why I had to endure such an awful span in my life. I could honestly answer, "No, I never did," and here is why. First, as a pastor, I have been bedside with many sick people, seeing them suffer and eventually die. I saw it so often I began to wonder, "Why not me? When would be my turn for this?" This is earth, not heaven. It is a fallen world. Bad stuff happens to people here.

Second, I've read the book of Job many times. Now, there was a brother who knew something about suffering. He continually asked God why he was suffering so and why he had to endure the endless bad theology of his friends' accusations that he must have committed some heinous sins to deserve this punishment.

Here it is in Job's own words. Job 13:1-5 (NIV).

> [1]"My eyes have seen all this, my ears have heard and understood it.
>
> [2] What you know, I also know; I am not inferior to you. [3] But I
>
> desire to speak to the Almighty and to argue my case with God.
>
> [4]You, however, smear me with lies; you are worthless physicians,
>
> all of you! [5] If only you would be altogether silent! For you, that

would be wisdom." (They didn't remain silent, by the way).

Job did argue his case with God, and God would give Job the answer to his question of "why." Job 38:1 begins with "Then the Lord answered Job out of the storm"(NIV). God would use four chapters, 129 verses to tell Job this one thing. "I am God, and I am sovereign." Period. Nothing more. God told Job how mighty, creative, wise, brilliant, fearless, awesome, and superior He was, and that was it.

Why, does God deliver what seems such a callous answer to the suffering Job's question of why? This is my personal opinion, but I'm writing the book, so I will take a little privilege here. I believe God answered in His way because in the long run it was more important for Job to know that God is sovereign than for him to know the reason for his terrible but temporary problems. I say this with all due respect to the Lord – God is large and in charge. He does what He does and does not owe an explanation to anyone. As difficult as it is to deal with it, it is still good.

Some suggest it is fine to ask God your why questions, and I won't take that privilege away. I've heard it said that doubt is your opportunity to exercise and grow your faith. It is thought that asking God why may be therapeutic. So ask the "why" question all you want but realize that He may not give you a clear and immediate answer to your question.

Now, let's rush to the most benevolent part of God's revelation. God is not only sovereign, He is also good. Good beyond measure. Hitler was sovereign over the minds and direction of Germany, but he wasn't good in his nature or his actions. God is both totally in charge of the universe, and to our great benefit, He is so good. Otherwise, he fits the mold of the gods and goddesses of ancient Greece and Rome, who had to be appeased constantly; and if a follower wanted something from them, he had to hope he asked when they were having a good day.

In August of 2021, I ran into a friend I hadn't seen since before I fell ill. We did a little catching up, then he asked me to pray for a friend of his who was in the hospital in critical condition from Covid. I promised to do so and did. I didn't see my friend again for about two months. Naturally, when we met again, I asked about his sick friend. He told me his friend had died. My friend said in trying to encourage the family during the illness, he told them to "pray and believe, pray and believe". After the death, a family member asked my friend, "So, what are we supposed to believe now?" He replied, simply but wisely, "God is sovereign."

I believe if you can't make peace with that truth, then you will never have peace with God. Yes, life may throw you some heart-breaking stuff, but you can't let go of the knowledge that despite the fact you don't understand what God is doing, God knows exactly what He is doing. He is infinitely smart, and I don't know about you, but I want a God who is smarter than me, a great deal smarter than me.

R.C. Sproul lays it out for us. "If there is one single molecule in this universe running around loose, totally free of God's sovereignty, then we have no guarantee that a single promise of God will be fulfilled."

I don't believe God doesn't always reveal the reasons for His actions because He is smug and resents being questioned. It may be that our questions about His will and His actions don't get answered to our satisfaction because it isn't our time to know. If it needs to be revealed, God will reveal it only at the proper time.

God also may choose not to reveal the reason for His actions because we wouldn't understand. God is so much grander in His knowledge and wisdom that we aren't able to grasp all His ways. It would be like a college physics professor giving a lecture to a kindergarten class. Zoom! Over their little heads. God could lay it all out for us and the best we could respond with would be, "Huh?"

English poet and author, Evelyn Underhill tells us, "If God were small enough to be understood, He would not be big enough to be worshipped."

Find assurance in the fact that God is sovereign, and He has this whole thing completely planned. Did it ever occur to you that nothing occurs to God? He knows it all because He created it all.

I must confess that during my illness and recovery, I did ask God the "why" question one time. After I came home in June of 2021, a sweet lady named Karen Pittman saw our story on one of the Oklahoma City news stations. She contacted us and asked if I would call her husband, Jerry, who was going through a situation very similar to mine. I called Jerry and we visited, sharing "war stories" about what we had been through and where we hoped we were going. He promised to come visit our church when he recovered, and I promised to stay in touch with him.

One week I sent him a text, but Karen answered the text telling me that Jerry was back in the hospital and not doing well. Her next text said Jerry had a new doctor and some new treatments and was responding. The next week, she texted to say Jerry had passed away. I had never met the man, but I cried like a baby over his death and her sorrow.

Then came my "why" question. "Why, God, did you not spare Jerry? He has a wife and family that love him and wanted to spend more days with him just like I am able to spend more days with mine. Why not spare him?"

God's answer to me was the same answer He gave to Job. "I am sovereign."

And I had to accept that. I still cried. His family still grieved. But a good God had made His decision, and it was our place to accept it. His answers may not always be pleasing to us, but they are always best for us. It doesn't require us to be able to understand Him to make His answers best.

Job finally got it. In Job 42:1-6 (MSG), he makes his confession.

> "I'm convinced: You can do anything and everything. Nothing and
>
> no one can upset your plans. You asked, 'Who is this muddying the
>
> water, ignorantly confusing the issue, second-guessing my
>
> purposes?' I admit it. I was the one. I babbled on about things far beyond
>
> me, made small talk about wonders way over my head. You told me, 'Listen, and let me do the talking. Let me ask the

Tony Peake 111

questions. *You* give the answers.' I admit I once lived by rumors of you; now

I have it all firsthand—from my own eyes and ears! I'm sorry—forgive me.

I'll never do that again, I promise! I'll never again live on crusts of hearsay,

crumbs of rumor."

Let's ask Jesus about the why question. He addresses it in Luke 13:1- 5.

"[1] About this time Jesus was informed that Pilate had murdered

some people from Galilee as they were offering sacrifices at the

Temple. [2] "Do you think those Galileans were worse sinners than

all the other people from Galilee?" Jesus asked. "Is that why they

suffered? [3] Not at all! And you will perish, too, unless you repent of

your sins and turn to God. [4] And what about the eighteen people

who died when the tower in Siloam fell on them? Were they the

worst sinners in Jerusalem? [5] No, and I tell you again that unless you

**repent, you will perish, too."**

Jesus deeply wants us to know the "why question" isn't nearly as important as the "what question." What are we to do when bad things happen to good people?

He says to repent. Something is going to take you out of this world, then all the "why questions" of earth won't matter. The ONLY THING that is important is that you confessed your sins and committed your life to Jesus. Because in the end, God is sovereign and will judge where our residence for eternity will be.

If you have an urgent request of God for a sick friend or family member, or any other time of critical circumstances, it is your job to pray and ask of Him. It is God's job to answer in His sovereign wisdom. So, understand it or not, like it or not, your job is to pray and keep praying. Then, as my pastor friend, Dr. Justin Dunn once told me, "Walk in the light you've been given." Take the knowledge and revelations God has given you and move on.

Let's do the same good work that Job did. Let's acknowledge and find peace in the fact that God is sovereign, and He is good.

**God is great, and I am grateful that He is sovereign.**

# CHAPTER 13

# Keep Your Eye on the Prize

*The Encouragement of the Reward of Heaven*

Alicia believed the best decision for me was to go to a rehab unit in Epworth Skilled Nursing Center in Oklahoma City, which had accepted me. It was time to move on from the only hospital setting that I remembered, the site where my trach tube was able to be taken out and my breathing began to take a turn for the better.

*Monday, March 29*

*Lisa, the physical therapist, came by (to say goodbye) and was so sentimental about him leaving. Tony was with her the day he began his crash. She told us how she went into another room and cried because she was scared, she had pushed him to hard (causing the crash) and he was going to die.*

Lisa made me promise that when I recovered, I would come back to visit her, walking in Select unassisted, good as new. I promised to although I couldn't conceive ever being able to walk, much less walk unassisted. But I did recover, and Alicia and I kept that promise when we visited Lisa and our first case manager, Beth Leonard, on Presidents' Day, 2022, in the lobby of Select Specialties Hospital.

I left Select Specialties at 3:30 p.m., Tuesday, March 30, 2021, to a sweet and rousing send-off by members of the hospital staff who lined the hallway and cheered us on as we left. I had progressed to the point that I was able to completely raise my arm and give them all a tip of my St. Louis Cardinals cap as we left.

Wednesday, March 31, arrived with my new wound doctor, Dr. Bell, coming by to "debride" the wound. I received a full assessment from the speech therapist, physical therapist, and occupational therapist. There may have even been a "How You Doing?" therapist in there somewhere.

I entered the hospital in Shawnee with a full goatee. I had undergone various stages of facial hair in that time, but finally decided to have a clean shave and be done with it. The staff willingly and skillfully obliged.

Thursday, April 1, I received some of the best therapy I could have received. The 2021 Major League Baseball season opened, and the Cardinals beat the Cincinnati Reds 11-6! A breath of fresh air of normalcy again. Life would indeed go on.

Well, it was de ja vu' all over again. On Friday, April 2, my breathing was extremely labored to the point an ambulance was called, I was taken to the emergency room at Mercy Hospital in Oklahoma City and intubated for a second time during my hospital days. Although I don't remember much about the ride, this was the first ambulance ride to this point that I at least remembered to some degree.

The reason for my setback was never definitely determined, but the best guess was I had aspirated while at Epworth. No one's fault, just some more of my crazy life. I was assessed and moved to the ICU Room 8 at Mercy which would be my home for the next four days.

I received an unexpected blessing in ICU. Hospital beds are made for functionality, and not much else. Comfort is a word that escapes their engineering and construction, but in ICU I was placed on something called a sand bed.

You have probably heard people state that if heaven is all about lying around on a cloud and playing a harp all day, they really didn't want to go. Well, I don't know about the harp part, but if heaven's clouds feel as comfortable as a sand bed, count me in for eternity!

What is a sand bed you ask? According to ETHOSOUTCOMES.COM, a sand bed, better known as an AFT, (Air Fluidized Therapy) is filled with silicone coated microspheres which resemble white sand. Warm air forced upward through these microspheres creates a dynamic fluid-like state. This fluid support optimizes immersion and envelopment, conforming to the irregularities of the body.

Those babies are beyond comfortable and are like paradise for a bed sore embattled wound patient, but they are not thought to be in the best interest of patients with lung and breathing difficulties, a.k.a., me. The sand bed was wonderful for my brief time in ICU, but I would never experience one again.

One afternoon in ICU, I received a wakeup call from reality. Outside the window of my room, I heard the low drone of an engine which became louder and louder. After reaching a crescendo, it then faded out of ear shot. What could that be? Soon the whole process started over. Louder and louder, then fade to silence. It finally dawned on me that it was April and the sound I was hearing was a lawnmower! I entered the hospital in November among the dead grass of winter, but now lawns were turning green, and the mowing season had begun again. Another semblance of normalcy in just three days! Maybe April would turn out to be better than I imagined.

Sunday, April 4, 2021, was Easter Sunday - a high point in the life of a Christian, a church, and certainly a pastor. Back in First Baptist, Tecumseh, the congregation would celebrate our Savior's resurrection in the capable of hands of Pastor Larry Sparks who was serving as interim pastor in my absence. He is a fine preacher and would fill the pulpit well, but I would miss another holiday, the holiday of all holidays.

As one who practically saw his life resurrected, I had a new appreciation for what God did for us that first Easter morning when he tossed aside the large stone closure in front of Christ's tomb with the ease you and I might use to flick off a piece of lent from one's clothing.

If you recall, my first desire of this book is to glorify our God. The second one is to offer hope to those who might be desperately in need of it. There is no greater hope than that found in Christ's resurrection.

I once heard a sermon from a preacher concerning the resurrection who offered this encouragement. When one of his children came to him with a problem he felt was bigger than life, he would begin the conversation by asking the simple but profound question, "Is the tomb still empty?" If the tomb is still empty, there is hope. He could then help his children work their way through whatever was bothering them. But if the tomb was no longer empty, the greatest hope of all hopes were shattered into a million dreadful pieces, and no hope beyond that is promised.

Stop for a moment and contemplate what crisis might be smothering you. What difference does it make in your time of trouble that the tomb is still empty? I hope you realize that the empty tomb makes all the difference in the world.

When I was in my first job as boys' basketball coach at Roff High School in Roff, Oklahoma, Rick Eaton, the veteran girls' basketball coach there, offered me this pearl of wisdom regarding the potential fragility of a coach's job. Rick said, "Remember, Tony, the worst thing they can do to you is the best thing they can do to you." He meant if I was ever fired from a position, I then had a chance to find another position where the conditions and the reception by the school and community would be much improved.

A similar thing happens in life. What do most feel is the worst thing that can happen to a person? Death. But for the Christian, death means the beginning of true life! The apostle Paul knew that so well that he proclaimed in Philippians 1:21 NLT, "For to me, living means living for Christ, and dying is even better." The worst thing life can do to a follower of Christ is the best thing it can do to a follower of Christ!

As one of God's Miracle Men, I received multiple chances at staying alive, but one day, I will have used up all my chances. Does that mean, on my final day, I lose? Heaven's no! I now get heaven!

Evangelist Dwight L. Moody knew this full well, and it inspired him to say,

> "Someday you will read in the papers, 'D. L. Moody of East Northfield is
>
> dead.' Don't you believe a word of it! At that moment I shall be more alive
>
> than I am now; I shall have gone up higher, that is all, out of this old clay
>
> tenement into a house that is immortal -- a body that death cannot touch,
>
> that sin cannot taint; a body fashioned like unto His glorious body. I was
>
> born of the flesh in 1837. I was born of the Spirit in 1856. That which is born
>
> of the flesh may die. That which is born of the Spirit will live forever."
>
> (*WWW.WHOLESOMEWORDS.ORG*)

Remember the story of Jesus raising the cold as a cucumber Lazarus from the dead and his grave? It was a miraculous work of the Lord which bore more evidence that He was the Messiah and afforded Lazarus and his sisters, Mary and Martha, more great time to spend together.

Not to be irreverent, but I would like to have read the headlines had Lazarus been interviewed by the *Bethany Gazette* on his return. The headlines might have read, "Local Man Rises from the Dead. Calls It a 'Bummer.'" Lazarus had it made in heaven's shade (It is just an expression. I know

God and Christ illuminate heaven so well there is no shade. Just work with me).

The resurrection of Lazarus glorified the Lord and caused many to believe in Him. John 12:11 (NLV), "Because of Lazarus, many Jews were leaving their own religion. They were putting their trust in Jesus." But Lazarus paid a price for all the good that was done. He had to leave the realization of his greatest earthly hope – heaven.

I say all that to say this. Jesus said that in this world you would have many troubles, and I'm sure you can attest that He is right. I would not for a minute want to trivialize your pains, problems, and predicaments. They are real and they hurt, but you must keep your eyes on the prize – the great hope of heaven.

Shadrach, Meshach, and Abednego defied the decree of King Nebuchadnezzar to bow down and worship a huge golden image of him. They would bow and worship only the One True God. Here was their answer to the outraged king in Daniel 3:17-18 (NIV):

> "[17]If we are thrown into the blazing furnace, the God we serve is
>
> able to deliver us from it, and he will deliver us from Your
>
> Majesty's hand. [18] But even if he does not, we want you to know,
>
> Your Majesty, that we will not serve your gods or worship the image
>
> of gold you have set up."

King Nebuchadnezzar was so outraged he ordered the furnace be heated seven times hotter than usual to receive the three Jewish rebels. Now, you can bet your bottom bitcoin that those three were hoping God would spare them from roasting like chestnuts on an open fire. Who wouldn't? But their confidence in God gave them the ability to face a brutal death in exchange for a glorious eternity in God's heaven.

Look at it this way. Suppose you were given the chance to go on a dream vacation. The mountains, the beach, fine museums and dining in a big city, whatever your dream vacation might be. You are also gifted with a vacation of two weeks instead of the usual one week. Now the flight to your dream destination will take three hours, six hours round trip. That means that of the 336 hours of your vacation, six hours will be spent in travel. The remaining 300 hours will be spent in unadulterated fun!

Now of those 336 hours, which part of the trip will you give most of your attention, most of your joyful anticipation? Would it be the 300 hours of pleasure or the six hours of getting to and fro? The 300 hours, of course! So why is it that we give so much attention to our brief travel time on earth compared to the eternal time of endless pleasure in heaven?

Yes, I realize this earth is the only home you have ever known, so this is your only point of reference. But you must rise above that and find hope in the ultimate hope of heaven with the Lord.

Gaining such a mindset won't allow you to skip the grief of death, disease, bankruptcy, divorce, a wayward child, being victim of physical and sexual abuse, etc. But the hope of heaven will allow you to find strength in realizing as a follower of Christ, eventually everything will turn out well, more than well, and your life will be well for eternity.

***God is great, and I am grateful for the great hope of heaven!***

# CHAPTER 14

## Give and It Will Be Given

*The Encouragement from Giving*

On Wednesday, April 7, I was moved upstairs to the second floor of the Mercy Hospital which is rented from Mercy by a hospital group called AMG. We had nothing against moving back to Epworth, but Alicia felt it would be easier to take a gurney trip downstairs to the Mercy ER rather than an ambulance ride across town if I had to re-enter the emergency room.

Due to insurance restrictions that I didn't understand, but that Alicia had a firm handhold on, I could only stay in AMG for fifteen days; then I had to move to a different type of facility. It was back to the drawing board as to where I would land next.

We were blessed to have fantastic nurses everywhere we stayed, but some rose to the top due to their skills, heart, and specific opportunities to serve. One of those in AMG was Adrian. I was still battling gastrointestinal disturbances that were registering on the rector scale. Adrian was able to adjust my finicky stomach to the nutritional formula I was receiving and decide when the best time was to have the flow on and off. She also discovered one of my problems was dehydration, and she gave help to rectify that. In Alicia's journal she described Adrian as "absolutely fantastic." She was a blessing at a time when we needed a blessing.

April 8 was Wooly Removal Day. My hair stylist and church friend, Shiane Neiman, made the trip from Tecumseh, to give me my first haircut since entering the hospital. She was a sight for my sore eyes and such a blessing.

Wednesday, April 14, brought me a pleasant surprise, Dixie Doodle, the therapy dog! I petted her as long as they would let me. Dixie was one more welcome taste of normalcy.

Jaime was my new speech therapist and was in charge of deciding what I could and couldn't swallow. I told her I was craving an orange slush from a Sonic Restaurant. It is a summertime delicacy in Oklahoma. Jaime felt that drinking a slush was a little too ambitious for me at that point, but she had an idea of mixing orange soda with small ice chips as a substitute. Jaime told me she would be in Saturday afternoon to give the soda and ice a try.

The afternoon came and went, and I was a little disappointed that she hadn't made it in. But in the evening, here she came! She had been at a baseball game of a young family member but took the time afterward on her Saturday to come by. She even sneaked in wearing her jeans and t-shirt, not taking the time to put on scrubs. (Please don't tell the hospital fashion police. She was just being kind.)

I got my ice chips and soda, and though it wasn't an orange slush, it tasted fantastic. Rack up two tastes of normalcy in one week.

The best bet for my next journey seemed to be Stroud Regional Medical Center in Stroud, Oklahoma. Stroud is about fifty-eight miles up the Turner Turnpike east of Oklahoma City. Stroud is also only about a one-hour drive from our home in Tecumseh. Stroud is a smaller town and a smaller facility, but it had the rehab requirements I needed and the wound care doctor there, Dr. Baolien Tu, was highly recommended by many. And my wound was at a point it needed a highly recommended wound care doctor.

By Friday, April 9, it was time to pump the brakes on Stroud Regional. They currently didn't have a bed for me. However, they had a sister hospital in Anadarko, Oklahoma, which had an open bed and was also served by Dr. Tu.

Anadarko and was sixty miles southwest of Oklahoma City. Alicia would be a one and one-half hour drive from Tecumseh to visit me in my new hospital.

Reality told us that Alicia driving that far each day to visit me was bordering on insanity. Anadarko was our only choice, but the bitter reality was Alicia could visit only on the weekends. As already noted, the highlight of my days was her visits.

She was my caregiver, confidant, counselor, advocate, and biggest cheerleader.

It is here that I enter a topic that is difficult for me to adequately describe. At this point, Alicia and I had been married thirty-eight years. Thirty-eight good years.

We raised two sharp children and one of which had produced three wonderful grandchildren. Alicia was and is my best friend. The number of "I'm so mad, I'm not talking to you for days" arguments we had in that time could be counted on one hand, and still have a few free digits left over. We were blessed with a happy marriage. But the trials we had been through had cemented our love into one I still can't adequately put into words. We had a love on steroids. We went from the ground floor of marital bliss up to the penthouse of marital paradise. Lest I take this too far and go all Hallmark Channel on you, let's just say, we were crazy about each other and didn't like the prospect of not seeing each other daily.

But the Lord had provided a bed in Anadarko, so Anadarko it would be.

At this point in my writing, I am finishing the first volume of Alicia's first journal. She dedicated the last two pages to list the names of people, churches, and groups who donated everything from money, to restaurant gift cards, to running errands, to mowing our lawn back home. Her list had a grand total of 116 groups and names! How humbling to read of the many acts and gifts of love from so many people.

Dr. Luke records the words of Christ in Luke 6:38 (NIV), "Give, and it will be given to you. A good measure, pressed down, shaken together and running over, will be poured into your lap. For with the measure you use, it will be measured to you."

Our supporters were on the brink of a pressed down, shaken together, and running over blessing for their love and generosity toward us.

I don't believe the Lord gave us those words as an investment strategy. God loves a cheerful giver, not necessarily a giver with millionaire aspirations through religious financial ventures. Nevertheless, scripture does promise rewards for those who reward others.

What blessings do you suppose were pressed down, shaken together, and running over into the lap of the poor widow who gave all the money she possessed into the Temple treasury?

That great theologian, Winston Churchill (you can't see me, but my tongue is in my cheek at this point) spoke of the value of giving when he said, "We make a living by what we get, but we make a life by what we give."

It is strange how giving can have a therapeutic quality to it for the giver. When we give to help others, regardless of how much or how little we have, the dividends pour in; not necessarily monetarily, but definitely in the form of lifting our spirits.

I don't know how we would have survived without the generosity of people not only from our church, community, county and even parts far beyond. One day after returning home, we received a card in the mail with a return address from the state of Washington. Who could this be? We didn't know anyone in Washington.

We opened the card and read the most moving message ever from a teacher in Washington. It read,

> **Pastor T***ony,*
>
> *We were told about your health issues by Matthew Mahler, who attends your church while at college (Oklahoma Baptist University). We are students at a small Christian school and have*

*been praying for you these last several months. Each quarter we collect an offering during our weekly chapel service. This last quarter we chose you to receive this offering. We hope it helps with your medical expenses.*

*Mrs. Sarah Mahler*

There was a check inside that would have allowed us to purchase about 500 orange slushes (tempting, but we didn't)! Those children from that little Christian school exhibited such a spirit of love and giving for someone they had never met and probably never will.

Are you suffering from the malady of hopelessness on any level now? Would you care for a prescription to help with that? Here it is – give. Just give. You can decide on the size of the dosage based on what you have to give. Giving to someone in need takes your eyes off yourself and your problems and puts your focus on God, the Giver of every good and perfect gift that comes down from the Father of the heavenly lights.

**God is great and I am grateful He blesses us with the gift of giving.**

# SECTION IV

# BUZZING OFF TO THE BEE

# CHAPTER 15

# Jehovah Jireh

*The Encouragement of God's Provision*

Anadarko, Oklahoma, has a population of around 5,700 friendly people in the southwestern corner of the state. The name, Anadarko, is derived from the name of a band of the Caddo tribe called Nadaco. It means "bumblebee place." The town is the capital of three Native American tribes and claims the title, "Indian City, U.S.A." It is the home of the National Hall of Fame for Famous American Indians. And it would soon be my fifth new hospital home.

It was just prior to departing for Anadarko that Jehovah Jireh, the Great Provider, began to provide for us again. Alicia had looked at her amount of sick leave and visited with her principal at Tecumseh High School, Randy Dilbeck, to devise a plan whereby Alicia could use a combination of her sick leave while doing work she needed to do by computer online and be able to be with me for the rest of the school year. Mr. Dilbeck was so gracious in working with Alicia to give her the time she needed.

That plan meant that Alicia would be able to come with me to Anadarko. Now don't hear me say something I'm not saying. We will be forever grateful to the folks in Anadarko for all they did for us, but like our town of Tecumseh, Anadarko didn't have anything resembling a five-star hotel. And if they had, we couldn't have afforded it. We had purchased a used travel trailer in October 2020, the month before I got Covid. We hauled it home, had it winterized, and parked it, anticipating not using it until the next spring. But Alicia thought that if we could find a place around Anadarko to park the trailer, she would be able to stay in it for the duration of my time there.

Now, where to park it? God continued to provide through the wonder of social media (And you were wondering if there was any redemptive value in social media). Alicia had posted her plan to camp out in Anadarko if she could find a site for our trailer.

Just like that, Alicia received a private message from a woman named Sandra Boyles (formerly Sandra McWhirter). Alicia and Sandra grew up together at Chisholm Heights Baptist Church in Mustang, Oklahoma. Sandra's husband, Bobby, is pastor of a beautiful little country church, Longview Church, located high on a hill near Anadarko. It had a fantastic view of the rolling hills of southwestern Oklahoma. Sandra informed Alicia the church was just completing installing full hook-up sights on their church parking lot. She invited Alicia to bring the trailer there and stay free of charge. Jehovah Jireh!

Our son, Cody, and his friend, Remington Pope, hauled the trailer to the church and set it up on the parking lot. The trailer needed some repairs before moving it and even after it arrived. But good friend, David Williams, and a man from Elk City, Oklahoma, with a traveling trailer repair unit business came to the rescue. Once again, I would receive those daily visits with Alicia.

Tuesday, April 20, 2021, was moving day…again. We departed for Anadarko around 2 p.m. About all I remember from the ride was staring out the back of the ambulance with no view of the day except blue sky and trying to find comfort from my bedsore wound while lying on the rocking gurney.

Sometimes God places people in your life for less than a blink of the eye, but they are forever remembered. Nurse Tracie was one of those "blink of the eye" people for me. Here I was at a new hospital, new surroundings, new procedures. Familiarity was nowhere to be found. But Nurse Tracie was more than kind and reassuring as she began to get my vitals and help me settle into my new home, Room 210, Physicians Hospital, Anadarko, Oklahoma. I would never see her again. I believe she was a traveling nurse, and her time was up at that hospital. I was grateful she traveled my way for just one day.

April 22 arrived in full glory marking 150 consecutive days in hospitals.

Time and time again, when Alicia and I faced a challenge for which we could see no solution, or at least not a good solution, when we turned it over to God, He provided. Where would I go after SSM Shawnee, after Select Specialties, after Epworth, after Mercy, after AMG, and after Anadarko? God provided. How would I endure painful and lonely days? God provided. And how would Alicia and I deal with being separated when I went to Anadarko? God provided.

Understand though that God's provision may not be the way we want Him to provide. More than once, we were denied acceptance into our first choice of hospitals, but He provided us good experiences at each one we entered.

And it isn't all about us. In one hospital I was able to share the Good News of Jesus with one of the staff members. That person was a believer, and further conversations revealed a troubled and painful life in her early years. We were

able to talk and pray through some of the issues. That wouldn't have happened had I been admitted in our first choice of hospitals.

Be prepared that God's provisions may not occur on your timetable. But He provides every day in His way, which is always the best way for you.

I thrive on the words of Corrie Ten Boom. "Never be afraid to trust an unknown future to a known God."

Paul proclaims in Philippians 4:19 (NKJV),

> **"And my God shall supply all your needs according to His riches in glory by**
>
> **Christ Jesus."  Did God supply all of Paul's needs? Absolutely.  Even when**
>
> **Paul asked the Lord to remove that painful and mysterious thorn in his flesh.**
>
> **Yes, He did, but not in the way Paul expected.  God explained to Paul that**

even though the thorn was painful, it would be more painful should God

take away the thorn, resulting in Paul bringing upon himself the pain of

pride.

Here it is in 2 Corinthians 12:8-10 (NLT),

"⁸ Three different times I begged the Lord to take it away. ⁹ Each

time he said, "My grace is all you need. My power works best in

weakness." So now I am glad to boast about my weaknesses, so

that the power of Christ can work through me. ¹⁰ That's why I take

pleasure in my weaknesses, and in the insults, hardships,

persecutions, and troubles that I suffer for Christ. For when I am

weak, then I am strong."

Can you imagine Paul interviewing with a modern-day missionary board in hopes of being accepted as an international missionary?

"So, Mr. Paul, what would you say is your greatest strength?"

"My weakness."

"No, you misunderstood the question. What is your strength?"

"My weakness. When I am weak, then I am strong."

"Okay. I'm afraid to ask you what your greatest weakness is."

Maybe Paul would have made it to the mission field anyway.

Can you imagine what might have happened to the early church if Paul's ministry and letter writing had been derailed by pride? Paul only took pleasure in his weaknesses, insults, hardships, persecutions, and troubles because they led to his desired outcome, to spread the good news that Jesus can bring eternal life and joy to anyone who will follow Him. He endured temporary pain in exchange for a permanent paradise.

That great theologian, Garth Brooks (again, tongue in cheek) sings "Some of God's greatest gifts are unanswered prayers." Actually God will answer any of your prayers offered in humility and faith, but you must be willing to let Him answer them in His own way. Should God's answer be disappointing to you, just hang on and take a ride of faith to see where His answers will take you.

May we wrap up this chapter with the inspirational words from just the first verse and chorus of the song, "Faithful Now" by the group, *Vertical Worship*?

> **I am holding onto faith**
> **'Cause I know You'll make a way**
> **And I don't always understand**
> **And I don't always get to see**
> **But I will believe it, I will believe it**
>
> **'Cause You make mountains move**
> **You make giants fall**
> **And You use songs of praise**

To shake prison walls
And I will speak to my fear
I will preach to my doubt
That You were faithful then
You'll be faithful now

*God is great and I am grateful for His provision!*

# CHAPTER 16

# Reserve Your Place

*The Encouragement from Having Christ in Your Heart*

Soon after arriving in Anadarko, I began training, bladder training that is. For as long as I could remember, and even before I could remember, I had been on a catheter. To prepare the bladder for having the catheter removed, the catheter tube is clamped for about three hours, then unclamped for an hour, training the bladder to take over its normal functioning pattern.

Eventually the catheter was removed, and I was on my own. It was less than smooth sailing. My bladder would function for one to two days, then stop for several days. This required a nurse to do an ultrasound of my bladder to assess the volume of urine I was retaining. When the volume reached a certain level, and my bladder didn't discharge it, I received the blessing of something called a straight catheter or as they say in the business, "straight cath." The straight catheter, also called an intermittent catheter, is a soft, thin tube used to pass urine from the body. Straight catheters are only used one time and then thrown away. That sounds simple enough, right? Except the process of inserting and removing a straight cath was about as much fun as hugging a porcupine. Painful doesn't begin to adequately describe the process. I believe straight caths were used as a torture method in medieval times. This battle between my bladder and a straight cath would continue for two weeks or more.

On the nights I was successful in using the urinal and eliminating urine myself, I would call Alicia and tell her. I was like a toddler in potty training telling his mother, "Mommy, I made pee pee!" Victories come in strange packages.

Another concern revolved around the belief that Anadarko was to be my last stop before returning home. If we couldn't get my bladder to work correctly, I might have to go home with a long-term catheter. Not a pleasant prospect. But one day, my bladder decided to cooperate full time. Then it was on to the next challenge.

The second day after arriving at Anadarko, I was allowed to have peas, noodles, and cobbler, plus a glass of tea. The most precious sign of normalcy to date. I could chew food and swallow again. Bring on the steak!

Steak wasn't on the menu yet, but a bottle of protein drink was. My stomach was not yet desiring food as much as I had anticipated. For most meals it was a struggle to get down an adequate amount of food. For the healing of my bedsore wound I needed good amounts of protein. So, if I didn't finish at least fifty percent of a meal, especially the meat dish, I had to drink a bottle of protein supplement. The drink was very helpful and fairly tasty, but it got old after a while. To this day I can't look a bottle of that stuff in the eye without shuddering.

Alicia was granted extended visitation hours of 2 to 6 p.m. On Friday, April 23, she hatched a plan for a special ops mission to sneak an orange slush in for me. But the Sonic in Anadarko didn't serve orange, so I settled for grape. Oh, the miseries I suffered.

What trials and trauma I experienced with no orange slush were quickly erased the next day by a "window visit" from Kaitlyn, and grandchildren, Jordy, Jaybea, and Johnny. Visitation rules at the hospital at that time wouldn't allow them to come in my room, which I totally understood. So, they came to my hospital room window. Alicia rolled my bed over to the window and we had a great visit.

Wednesday, April 28, was the big day the nurses came to my room to remove the food tube from my stomach. It took two of them to pull it out, but I finally was free. In time the opening in my upper stomach healed and left an indention that looked like a belly button. It was about four inches above my actual belly button.

After arriving back home, we got to see our grandchildren. I pulled up my t-shirt and told Johnny, "Look, I have two belly buttons!" He gave me one of those "Okay, I know you don't have two, but I still don't know what is going on" looks.

I tell people my actual belly button is from being born. The pseudo-belly button must be from when I was born again. Actually, I was born again up and to the left - in my heart.

From my teaching days, I had a copy of a textbook that I used to teach anatomy and physiology. When Kaitlyn was about six years old, she and I were looking through the textbook. I would show her diagrams of different parts of the body (Okay, it wasn't "Goldilocks and the Three Bears", but

Tony Peake 143

I was trying). When we got to the heart diagram, I pointed out the four chambers and how they worked. Kaitlyn then asked me, "Which part of the heart is where Jesus lives?" A fair question.

In the ancient Middle East, the seat of emotions was thought to be in the intestines. So, when it comes to making the decision concerning following Christ, I guess you have to trust your gut.

And that would be a great decision to make for a variety of reasons but let me share a compelling one you may not have given much thought. I recently was reading about the horrible regime of Saddam Hussein and his sadistic sons, Uday and Quasay. Uday was considered to be the more sadistic of the two brothers. Can you imagine being so evil that other evil people notice?

According to history.com,

> "Uday continued to make a name for himself among the Iraqi
>
> people for his sadism and cruelty. Prone to beating and torturing his
>
> servants and anyone else who displeased him, he was known to
>
> spend time studying new torture devices and methods to improve
>
> his technique. He even treated his so-called friends poorly—in one
>
> report, he forced some to drink dangerous amounts of alcohol

> purely for his amusement. Uday was also a man of unrestrained
>
> sexual appetites, sleeping with several women per night up to five
>
> nights a week. He was known for raping young women—some as
>
> young as 12—whom he found attractive, threatening their and their
>
> families' lives if they complained or spoke out against the crime. He
>
> would sometimes torture and kill his victims after sex.

Pretty sick, huh? But grab hold of this. We see no evidence that the Husseins ever accepted Christ as their Lord and Savior. As a result, the Bible would tell us in John 3:18 NIV, "Whoever believes in him is not condemned, but whoever does not believe stands condemned already because they have not believed in the name of God's one and only Son." That condemnation is an eternity separated from God in a real (and awful) place called hell. Now that is torture.

Stay with me. James 2:10 (NLT), explains to us, "For the person who keeps all of the laws except one is as guilty as a person who has broken all of God's laws." We have to believe that the Husseins went to hell for their wickedness and depravity. They broke God's law and did not ask for His forgiveness. We all have broken God's law and without asking for His forgiveness and committing to live your life for Christ, we are destined to hell. So, if you aren't a born-again believer in Jesus Christ, among your neighbors for your eternity in hell will be the Husseins. Is that the neighborhood you want to live in forever?

Who sits on the throne of your heart? Who is your Lord and Savior? Leave the horror of hell behind and reserve your place that Jesus promised for you in His Father's mansion.

***God is great and I am grateful for the saving grace of Jesus!***

# CHAPTER 17

## Do You Want to Get Well?

*The Encouragement of Hard Work and Persistence*

By this time, my wound doctor, Dr. Tu, had hooked me up to a wound vac, also known as a vacuum assisted closure. A wound vac is used as a therapeutic technique using a suction pump, tubing and a dressing to remove excess cellular waste to enhance healing in acute wounds. It uses a bleach-like solution called Dakin. The wound vac circulates the solution for six minutes every two hours. The dead tissue is drawn into a reservoir to hold the waste which is disgusting to look at and even worse to smell, but it serves an important purpose.

In using a wound vac properly, the wound has to be bandaged to be airtight in order to assure the vacuum needed to operate the pump correctly. Should the bandage develop a leak, an alarm goes off to alert that the bandage is open in order that the bandage might be resealed. This seldom happened in the hospital; but it happened more frequently after I went home, and the alarm usually went off in the middle of the night! It's Murphy's Law of Wound Vacs.

The main wound vac is a bedside device, but there is a portable model for times it is necessary for the patient to leave the bed. That meant I was tethered to one 24/7. It was royal pain but so was the bedsore wound. Using it for several months was not fun for me and no picnic for Alicia either; but it was valuable to speed up the healing process. I didn't want it, but I certainly needed it.

The whole process reminds me of the story of Naaman in 2 Kings. Naaman was a man's man, a valiant and highly successful military leader in Aram. His victories brought great satisfaction and wealth to his king. His reputation and demeanor were so profound, he received admiration everywhere he went.

Naaman was particularly a thorn in the side of the countries of Israel and Judah. Historical rumor has it that it was Naaman's arrow that killed King Ahab (1 Kings 22:34-36).

So Naaman's life was very successful and satisfying except for the fact that he had leprosy. Leprosy was a skin disease with no known cure. It would eat away at body parts until finally killing its host.

Naaman's wife had a servant girl brought back from a raid in Israel. The girl had compassion on Naaman and told his wife that he should go see Elisha the prophet in her home turf of Samaria. The prophet would be able to call on her God and bring healing to Naaman.

The wife relayed the story to Naaman, and he wasted no time in going to the king to get his passport to enter Samaria. Evidently, this occurred during a time of peace between the countries. So Naaman packed a bag, gathered his entourage and made off to meet Elisha. He took along with him 900 pounds of gold and silver (Bible scholars think amounting to over a million dollars) along with a wardrobe of ten brand new outfits, all for Elisha (Copays were brutal back then).

Naaman pulls up to Elisha's house in his impressive chariot, expecting Elisha to come out and greet this great warrior, but Elisha basically phones it in. He sends a messenger to greet Naaman who gave him a prescription from Elisha for his leprosy. "Go wash seven times in the Jordan River."

Outrage doesn't begin to describe Naaman's response. He fully expected a grand greeting from Elisha who would then call upon his God and he would be immediately healed. He left in his chariot in a huff, complaining that he had better rivers than the Jordan back home in which he could have washed.

Fortunately, a servant of Naaman's talked some sense into him, and he returned to Samaria. Second Kings 5:14 (MSG) tells us, "So he did it. He went down and immersed himself in the Jordan seven times, following the orders of the Holy Man. His skin was healed; it was like the skin of a little baby. He was as good as new." His healing was waiting there for him all along but had to follow the doctor's orders in order to receive it.

Or take the story of Jesus meeting the crippled man beside the pool at Bethesda.

The sick and afflicted gathered at the pool in hopes of receiving healing. It was believed that an angel would enter the water causing the pool to bubble. As the bubbles appeared, everyone rushed to get in the pool. The first person into the water would be healed. Last one in was a rotten

Tony Peake   149

egg, and so was everyone else except the lucky first diver. The crippled man had been at this for thirty-eight years failing to ever be first into the pool. He was 0 for 38. What a losing streak!

But in year thirty-nine, Jesus comes along and asks the crippled man a peculiar but pointed question. John 5:6 (NIV), "Do you want to get well?" Say what? He wasn't lying by the pool just to work on his suntan! But listen deeper into Jesus' question. "Do you really want to be healed? Are you willing to do whatever is needed to walk again?" Healing must be accompanied by a genuine desire to be healed.

If you are looking for a message of hope, here it is. Go jump in the Jordan, be the first into the pool, take the meds, do the physical therapy, go see the counselor, remove yourself from your toxic environment, submit your resignation letter, go back to school, learn a new skill, get help with your financial woes. As Nike says, "Just Do It!"

My wound vac was my albatross, but it wasn't around my neck. It was finally removed in September 2021. Yet, if I had refused the treatment, who knows how long my healing would have dragged on or what further damage it could have caused to my body? Early on, Dr. Tu feared that if we didn't get a grip on healing the wound, it would enter my spine, then I would really have problems. Thank God for the wound vac!

One of Abraham Lincoln's favorite phrases was, "This too shall pass." Somehow, some way, someday, God will bring peace to you in your current predicament. Romans 8:29 (NLT) speaks to this, "And we know that God causes everything to work together for the good of those who love God and are called according to his purpose for them."

God will either walk you through your trial to a better conclusion, he or walk you to a better way to live, if not flourish, within your trial.

***God is great and I am grateful for His healings!***

# CHAPTER 18

# Praise the Lord!

*The Encouragement of Unconditional Worship*

Thursday, April 29 was one of the days I was taken care of by Tech Jayla. Jayla would do anything for anyone, and she always did so with a smile. One evening, Alicia had spent most of the day with me and had helped me with most of my needs. Just before the end of shift, Jayla came in my room and began rubbing both of her eyes with her fists pretending to be drying her tears. I hadn't called for her help all afternoon and evening, and she was letting me know about it. What a sweetheart and provider.

More baby steps continued toward taking steps. On Friday, April 30, Physical Therapists Justin and Tori came in with a new challenge. They lifted me into a standing position, and I held on to the handles of a walker. I was asked to keep standing by my own power as long as I could. I lasted a grand total of ten seconds, two times. I felt like Hercules!

The early hours of Saturday, May 1, brought a new and painful challenge. I was awakened by a relentless burning sensation under my sternum. It lasted non-stop for about 90 minutes. The next day, the staff did an EKG on me which showed no signs of heart issues. It was thought to be acid reflux.

That turned out to be the case. I had been on an acid reflux medication for several years. As is customary, when I first entered the hospital in Shawnee, Alicia was asked to give a list of my current medications. The record of my medications would follow me from hospital to hospital. As the number of medications added grew, so did the length of my medication records.

When I entered Anadarko, they were unable to get my brand of acid reflux medication and a substitute medication wasn't provided. No one's fault. These things happen, but as a result my stomach was a ticking time bomb; and it exploded in the wee hours of May 1.

The episodes would continue, one to two times a day, again for about ninety minutes. The pains were so regular in length I could almost set my watch by them. And each time the pain would be constant. Chewable antacids weren't strong enough to have any effect, and although I had been given a new acid reflux medication, those take days to achieve full effectiveness. So when an episode would hit me, I would look at the clock on the wall and tell myself, "Tony, that minute hand will have to make one and a half trips around the face of that clock before you get any relief." My only recourse to deal with the pain was to clinch my fists, grind my teeth, and try to think of something that would help take my mind off the pain.

One evening I felt my gastral nemesis arrive and braced

myself for the one and one-half hour battle. After thirty minutes of clenched fists and grinding teeth, I spontaneously began to sing an inaudible hymn to myself. Then I sang another, and another, followed by another. I clinched, grinded, and sang every hymn I could recall. When I had exhausted my repertoire of hymns, I felt the pain beginning to subside. I looked at the clock and realized I had been singing for an entire hour. The Lord was praised and the pain was gone!

That was the good news, and I was grateful for it. Then it dawned on me that I had been walking this earth for over sixty years claiming to be a child of God, yet never once had I taken the time to praise the Lord for an entire hour. Isn't He deserving of that?

Now I routinely have mini-worship services, just the Lord and I. You see, we should worship the Lord and can worship the Lord regardless of our circumstances.

I once read a story shared online by Pastor John Ed Mathison. It involved a church from North Carolina who sent a mission team to a leper colony on the Caribbean Island of Tobago. The team met a lot of sad patients afflicted with leprosy. One memorable experience was a worship service that they held in the campus chapel.

The lepers came in and took their seats on the pews and the mission team led them in hymns. The pastor of the group was a man named Jack. He noticed that there was one leper on the back row who was facing in the opposite direction. All the rest of the lepers were facing the song leader.

Jack announced, "We have time for one more hymn. Does anyone have a favorite?" About this time the leprous lady on the back row turned around and for the first time faced the song leader. Jack said that it was the most hideous site that he had ever seen in a human being. She had no nose or lips. Her head was almost like a skull. When she raised her arm in the air, she had no hand. It was just a nub.

The pastor then reported that this leprous lady asked, "Could we sing 'Count Your Many Blessings'?" It was at that point that the whole mission team experienced something that they had never experienced before that was beyond description.

Here was a lady, with relatively nothing to be thankful for, asking to sing "Count Your Many Blessings." At first they couldn't even lead the song, but then they sang it with a profound new meaning.

Another source of the story reports that after returning home to North Carolina, the pastor was sharing the story with a friend. The friend commented, "I bet you will never sing that song again." The pastor replied, "Yes, I will sing it again, but in an entirely different way."

Imagine yourself sitting in a jail cell in a foreign country with your feet secured in stocks. You are there simply for sharing the good news of Jesus with those who didn't know it, but desperately needed it. The Apostle Paul and his missionary trip companion, Silas, could imagine such a scenario because that is exactly what happened to them.

It was on Paul's second missionary journey that he traveled to Philippi in Macedonia or modern day Greece. He was joined by Silas, young Timothy, and perhaps Dr. Luke. Philippi was "the place where the armies of Mark Antony and Octavian defeated Brutus and Cassius in the decisive battle of the second Roman civil war in 42 B.C." (Hughes) Because of this, many Roman soldiers retired in the area, and Philippi was proud of its Roman connection. (*Enduring Word Commentary*)

Paul sought out a place to share the gospel there, and he found one down by the river. He found a group who were worshippers of God, but not familiar with the redemptive story of Christ. Paul shared Christ's story with them. A woman in the fashion business named Lydia and members of her household gladly accepted Christ as their personal Savior and were baptized there in the river. They didn't even have to wait to fill and heat the baptistery!

Sometime later, Paul and Silas were being followed by a slave girl with demonic spirit who made her masters a good living by fortune-telling. She followed them throughout the city for several days. I suppose Paul was unable to get a restraining order against her, so he commanded, in the name of Christ, that the demonic spirit leave her. And the spirit complied.

The masters of the girl were furious because Paul's healing of the girl caused them to lose their meal ticket. The masters gathered a crowd and incited a riot, beating Paul and Silas. Naturally, Paul and Silas were arrested and put in the city jail. I guess that saying, "No good deed goes unpunished" was valid in this case.

Now, you may know the rest of the story, and it is a good one. Paul and Silas were set free from their stocks, and the cell doors flew open by the force of an earthquake registering maybe a seven on the Richter scale.

The jailer woke in a panic thinking all the prisoners had

escaped and planned his death in order to avoid the severe punishment from his supervisors for losing those under his watch. Paul reassured him that all prisoners were present and accounted for. The jailer asked Paul what he needed to do to be saved – not saved from his supervisors, but saved from his sins.

The jailer and his family received forgiveness in Christ, were baptized, and invited Paul and Silas over to his place to celebrate his family's salvation. What a story! What an ending!

We can never discount the value of lost souls receiving Christ as did the jailer and his family, but there is another story here. Hit the rewind button to the time before the earthquake shook the place.

There, stop rewinding right there. We see the two missionaries sitting in stocks in jail. Are you imagining yourself in a similar predicament, bound in the stocks of your troubles? If so, what would be your reaction to your dilemma? Demand to see a lawyer? You certainly would be deserving of one. Contact an investigative reporter from the local news channel to tell your story so that the news of this injustice could be spread? The public has a right to know. How about conducting a sing-along of your favorite hymns? Maybe not.

But that is exactly how Paul and Silas passed the time in a crummy Philippian jail cell. Acts 16:25 (NIV), "About midnight Paul and Silas were praying and singing hymns to God, and the other prisoners were listening to them." They sang their little missionary hearts out! And the other prisoners listened as they praised their God.

I hope you see the hope that can be found in worshipping

God even in the middle of your biggest problems. If your worship of God is based solely on emotions, then worshipping Him during tough times may not happen.

Such was not the case for David in Psalm 42:5 (MSG), "Why are you down in the dumps, dear soul? Why are you crying the blues? Fix my eyes on God—soon I'll be praising again. He puts a smile on my face. He's my God."

A vital part of your arsenal for battling tough times in your life should be praising God. Stop what you are doing now, think of a song that glorifies the greatness of God, and lift it all the way to heaven's gates. Sing to your heart's content because praising God will make your heart content.

*God is great, and I am grateful I can worship Him no matter my circumstances!*

# CHAPTER 19

## Cry Me A River ⋯ And Laugh Me One Too

*The Encouragement from Laughing and Crying*

Tuesday, May 4, Occupational Therapist Allison and Physical Therapist Tori came for my therapy session. I played volleyball with Tori using a big red balloon. I even made an outstanding play with my foot when the balloon was returned to me too low to hit with my hand. Atta kid!

On the morning of Thursday, May 6, as part of my physical therapy, I puttered down the hallway in a wheelchair to the scales to be weighed. The scales revealed I weighed in a whopping 164 pounds. That was a great fighting weight providing my opponent was nothing more than my shadow.

I also did another session of seeing how long I could stand while supporting myself with a walker. During three sets, I managed to remain standing for fifty, thirty-five, and twenty-two seconds. That was a new personal indoor record!

Sunday, May 9, was Mother's Day. Just like Valentine's Day,

I had nothing to give Alicia. To top it off, Cody was working in Wyoming, and Kaitlyn was at a hospital in Sherman, Texas, with Jackie who was having his appendix removed. Man, our family really knows how to do holidays. But Alicia's sister, Tracie, and fiancé, Cody, made a window visit at the hospital and brought lemon cookies to salvage at least part of the day.

Physical therapy on Monday, May 10, consisted of leg lifts, knee squeezes, and heel lifts hopefully to help strengthen my feet and toes. I had developed "drop foot" from being in a hospital bed so long, my toes were curled under and my feet were pointed downward. We are told the toes are one of the last body parts to recover.

My emotions had been on a hiatus for a while. When I was in a regular room at Select, I realized one day that I had never laughed since I woke up in late January. That wasn't necessarily because of depression or I was throwing myself an ongoing pity party. It just seemed like my brain cells never discussed the topic of humor at their daily staff meetings. In time though, I began making jokes with the nurses. By that, Alicia knew I was getting better.

But another emotion kicked in on May 10. I cried. It was the first time I had cried since I could remember. I had plenty to cry about before that day, but crying didn't seem to be a topic at my brain cells staff meetings either. But that day, the dam broke and I cried like a professional onion peeler. And I haven't stopped.

I don't cry continuously, but I cry often. And I cry over anything. I cry when I see a butterfly. I cry when I see a puppy. I cry when I see a tractor. The motivation for crying doesn't seem to matter. I cry.

My sister, Sunny Jo, was hospitalized with Covid-19 for two months in the summer of 2021. Covid seems to have an affinity for the Peak clan. After she was released from the hospital, she and I were visiting over the phone, comparing our battles and symptoms. I asked her if she cried a lot. She said she cried all the time. Because Covid does some strange things, we were pinning our tears on the evil virus.

When I would have opportunities to share the story of what God has done in the lives of Alicia and I, I would begin each time with the disclaimer that I, in all likelihood, would cry at some point in my message. I asked the group to bear with me. I would pull it back together and carry on.

On November 30, 2021, then again on December 2, I had the extreme privilege of speaking to a group of nurses from SSM Hospital in Shawnee. By this time I had shared the story several times with other gatherings, and I thought on this day I probably could get through it without crying. I was big and brave now. But when Alicia and I entered the meeting room where I would speak, she began to introduce me to some of the nurses who had taken care of me, because I didn't remember them or anything from my time in Shawnee. I began crying as I thanked each one of them. I couldn't even make it to the podium to speak before the water works began. The big and the brave quickly became the wimpy and the weepy.

According to *medicalnewstoday.com*, crying can be beneficial in several ways.

Crying can have a soothing effect. It can help you regulate emotions and reduce stress. Crying can help to relieve pain and improve mood. Shedding emotional tears releases oxytocin and endorphins, chemicals which make people feel good. Crying releases toxins and relieves stress. Crying helps to kill bacteria and keep the eyes clean as tears contain a fluid called lysozyme, an antimicrobial fighter.

Another benefit of crying is it makes you more Christlike. The Bible records an occasion when Jesus cried. This occurred at the death of His close friend, Lazarus, in Bethany. After greeting Jesus, Martha, a sister of Lazarus, found his other sister, Mary, to tell her Jesus had arrived.

> **John 11:32-35 (NIV), "[32] When Mary reached the place where Jesus was and**
>
> **saw him, she fell at his feet and said, 'Lord, if you had been here,**
>
> **my brother would not have died.' [33] When Jesus saw her weeping,**
>
> **and the Jews who had come along with her also weeping, he was**
>
> **deeply moved in spirit and troubled. [34] 'Where have you laid him?' he asked.**
>
> **'Come and see, Lord,' they replied.**
>
> **[35] Jesus wept."**

Verse 35 is important for more reasons than it gives children a quick and easy verse to memorize for Sunday School. It demonstrates that we have a Lord who cares when we hurt and grieve. Satan will do his best (or worst, which is his best) to convince you otherwise. He wants you to believe that God is distant and uncaring, that He is a God who can't be depended on in your times of sorrow.

There is a good Greek term for that, "hog wash." If you don't think God cares, then grab your Bible and black out all the writings in the Gospels about Jesus' torture, His crucifixion, and His resurrection. If the cross doesn't convince you that God cares for you, then you may be inconvincible.

The next time Satan shows up with his lies about God's lack of love for you, give him a one-word response, "Golgotha." The hill of the skull is a monument to the truth that "For God so loved the world that he gave his one and only Son, that whoever believes in him shall not perish but have eternal life" (John 3:16 NIV).

Jesus shedding tears happened again and occurred just outside Jerusalem. The instance is recorded in John 19:41-44 (ESV),

> "**41 And when he drew near and saw the city, he wept over**
>
> **it, 42 saying, 'Would that you, even you, had known on this day**
>
> **the things that make for peace! But now they are hidden from**
>
> **your eyes. 43 For the days will come upon you, when your enemies**
>
> **will set up a barricade around you and surround you and hem you**
>
> **in on every side 44 and tear you down to the ground, you and your**

**children within you. And they will not leave one stone upon another**

**in you, because you did not know the time of your visitation."'**

In Bethany, Jesus wept over the sorrow of the death of Lazarus. In Jerusalem, Jesus wept over the sorrow of death for those who were rejecting Him as their Savior. We should be happy over things that make Jesus happy, and we should grieve over the things that make Jesus grieve.

We are told in Romans 12:15 that Christians are called to a ministry of laughing and crying. "[15] Rejoice with those who rejoice, and weep with those who weep."

There are two occasions when you can build and cement relationships, when you laugh with someone, and when you cry with someone.

There is a scene from the movie, *Quigley Down Under* when Crazy Cora, played by Lora San Guicomo, is trying to console a crying aborigine baby while hiding from the bad guys bent on killing them. Recalling a sad time in her past when she tried to suppress the crying of her own baby, Cora responds, "That's it baby, cry. Cry, (expletive deleted) let's both make some noise!"

There will be times when you need to take the advice of Crazy Cora, "Baby, cry!"

Sure, there are times you will have to hold it together as best as you can, but there are also times you should take a cue from the wisest man in history, King Solomon, who encourages you with, "[1] To every thing there is a season, and a time to every purpose under the heaven … [4] A time to weep, and a time to laugh; a time to mourn, and a time to dance", (Ecclesiastes 3:1,4 KJV).

Do you need to make a time to cry? Not tears of hopelessness, but tears of plain old pain. Yes, God is with you. Yes, God will hold you. Yes, God will carry you through your trying times. But tears of pain are just additional prayers to God concerning how much you need Him in that moment.

If we continue our search for support from Scripture, we discover there is only one location in which you will never cry over your pain and problems, and it lies in the words of Revelation 21:1-5,

> "¹Then I saw 'a new heaven and a new earth,' for the first heaven
>
> and the first earth had passed away, and there was no longer any sea.
>
> ² I saw the Holy City, the new Jerusalem, coming down out of heaven
>
> from God, prepared as a bride beautifully dressed for her husband.
>
> ³ And I heard a loud voice from the throne saying, 'Look! God's dwelling
>
> place is now among the people, and he will dwell with them. They will
>
> be his people, and God himself will be with them and be their God.
>
> ⁴ *'He will wipe every tear from their eyes. There will be no more death'*ᵗ

Tony Peake 167

*or mourning or crying or pain, for the old order of things has passed*

*away."* **(Italics mine). ⁵ He who was seated on the throne said, "I am**

**making everything new!" Then he said, "Write this down, for these**

**words are trustworthy and true."**

What is trustworthy and true? The fact that the only place in the world where you will never cry tears of pain and anguish is in God's new heaven and new earth. And you ain't there yet, so be prepared to cry.

When the season comes for "a time to weep", weep yourself to a better place.

And one of those seasons it is so appropriate for you to weep is when you sing rich lyrics like:

> When I survey the wondrous cross
> On which the Prince of glory died,
> My richest gain I count but loss,
> And pour contempt on all my pride.
>
> Forbid it, Lord, that I should boast,
> Save in the death of Christ my God!
> All the vain things that charm me most,
> I sacrifice them to His blood.
>
> See from His head, His hands, His feet,
> Sorrow and love flow mingled down!
> Did e'er such love and sorrow meet,
> Or thorns compose so rich a crown?

Were the whole realm of nature mine,
That were a present far too small;
Love so amazing, so divine,
Demands my soul, my life, my all.

[x] Isaac Watts 1707, "When I Survey the Wondrous Cross", *Baptist Hymnal, #234.*

***God is great, and I'm grateful for His gift of laughter and tears!***

# CHAPTER 20

## Step by Step

*The Encouragement of Putting One Foot in Front of the Other*

From an early morning x-ray on Tuesday, May 11, it was discovered I had a spot on my lungs that was feared could be the start of pneumonia. So it was out of the bed and into the recliner for some vertical time for much of the day.

Hallelujah! Another sign of normalcy. Terri showed up that afternoon with banana pudding from Debra Fletcher. Debra even sent pudding and cookies for the nurses. Oh, it was good, and it reminded me so much of home. Doesn't banana pudding remind you of home?

Wednesday, May 12, 2021, was monumental. My strength, gained from standing by my bedside with the assistance of a walker, convinced Therapists Tori and Allison that I was ready to take my first steps since November 24, 2020 (I had taken a few steps with the aid of a sling back in Select, but I was basically floating and "touching down" with my feet).

Tori assisted me getting out of bed and on the walker. Allison told me to walk as far as I possibly could. When I grew too tired, she would be behind me with a wheelchair that I could sit in and recuperate. My first attempt at walking produced eight steps! If you are currently ambulatory, can you imagine that it would be difficult to walk only eight steps before pooping out? But that was the limit for me.

I took around four to five minutes to regain my breath, then I made a second attempt. I walked thirteen steps! I was shattering walking records left and right. But those combined twenty-one steps was all I had in me, and that was all my physical therapy for the day.

Allison had been coaching me how to sit up in bed by letting my feet fall off the side and using the momentum from my legs falling to lift me and to grab the guard rail on the bed to pull myself upright. After physical therapy, I reversed the process by sitting on the edge of the bed, falling sideways on the bed and using that momentum to pull my legs and feet back in bed. It would be a while before I could manage to get the legs and feet completely up without assistance, but we were getting there.

My second opportunity to go outside since being hospitalized went better than the first time at Select. It was now May 13, and the temperature was much more friendly for a man dressed in only a hospital gown than it was back in March. Alicia rolled me down the hallway in a wheelchair and onto the sidewalk on the north side of the hospital.

It was amazing! I saw clouds and houses and cars and trucks motoring up and down the street. I welcomed a glimmer of hope that daily normalcy might be a possibility for me.

That day brought another treat. Larry and Marilyn Lockard, along with Joy Bickers, members of our church, made a window visit. It was more than refreshing to see them. That was almost more normalcy than I could handle for one day. And yes, after they left, I cried.

On Friday, May 14, Lanny made a visit to Anadarko for the first time. It was so good to see him, and we talked about old times. I don't know if Anadarko, Oklahoma, qualified as Dixie, but "old times there were not forgotten," and actually were cherished.

On Monday, May 17, Therapists Justin and Tori stretched me out by walking me farther. I made it to the door of my room and a short ways down the hall to the left. Therapist Allison came that afternoon to begin teaching me how to get on the walker and over to the toilet chair, so I could begin to use it instead of a bedpan. That was the meager beginnings toward a day I longed for.

If I were to ask you what you might do today that would be personally exciting, I seriously doubt you would say, "To use the bathroom by myself." But that was a major goal for me. Some nights in my hospital bed I would longingly look toward the glow of the light in the bathroom. I would plot how I could slide out of bed, crawl to the bathroom, pull myself up with the handrail on the wall beside the toilet, do my business, then crawl back to my bed. Once there I would find a way to pull myself back up in bed. That was the point at which Dr. Reality made a house call and told me "There ain't no way, Jose." Personal potty time would have to wait until a much later date.

Attempts to get me walking again continued to improve. On Friday, May 21, I walked out of my room, turned left, and made it down a hallway of about seventy-five feet in length with only one rest break.

Saturday, May 22, saw one down and one up. The down was when a new occupational therapist, Keisha, came to work with me. Saturdays were usually off days, but she came in to give me a little extra work. She took me to the OT workout room, and asked me to stand to try some exercises, but every time I stood I got dizzy. So much for the extra OT.

The upside was Interim Pastor, Larry Sparks, requested Alicia and I make a video to address the congregation back in Tecumseh. Alicia and I made about three attempts at it before getting something worthwhile. She forwarded it to Larry and it was shown on the big screen in the worship service the next day.

Sunday morning, May 24, Alicia and I watched the live stream worship service from Tecumseh FBC. Then it was an afternoon of watching college softball and Cardinal baseball. The Cards lost to the Cubbies (Insert a frowning emoji here).

Monday, May 24, was a day of building confidence. Therapists Tori and Kelsey came to take me on my daily walk. But Tori said that the marching orders were for me to walk to the door, turn right, and begin walking down the longer, 150 foot hallway. She said the goal was for me to be able to go the entire length of the hallway by the end of the week. Rest breaks were allowed, but I had to make it all the way down the hallway by Friday.

I took my walker, made it out the doorway, lowered my head and lumbered down the hallway. With two rest breaks, I made it all the way down the hallway on Day One. Everyone was pumped, but I was too winded to offer a "Yippee!"

On day two and day three I pulled off the same feat. Justin and Tori fitted me with AFO braces which stands for Ankle Foot Orthosis. I'm not sure what orthosis means, but it is an impressive word. AFO braces are made of plastic and fit inside shoes, underneath the foot and up the back of the leg where they are strapped at the top of the calf muscle. With my toes curled under, getting the shoes and AFO braces on was the tough part. By comparison, walking was relatively easy.

The morning of May 27, I decided to grit my teeth and go as far as I possibly could go. About two-thirds of the way, I was still up and going. I passed the usual rest break point and carried on. I was tiring fast, but I heard Tori say, "You can rest if you need to, but you are crushing it, crushing it!" That was the boost I needed.

I went from walking eight steps on May 12 to walking 150 feet without stopping on May 26. After 185 days in hospitals, I struggled up the hallway and into a sense of greater hope for the future. Praise God from whom all blessings flow! Maybe someday I would walk unassisted again and keep my promise to Lisa at Select Specialties to walk back in and pay her a visit.

Hurray for Psalm 37:23 (ESV), "The steps of a man are established by the LORD, when he delights in his way."

**God is great and I am grateful for directing my steps!**

# CHAPTER 21

## Great Is Thy Faithfulness

*The Encouragement of God's Daily Mercies*

Wednesday afternoons were staff assessment days. Designated members of the hospital staff would discuss the progress and procedures for each patient. An unthinkable proposal came out of the meeting Wednesday, May 26. There was a chance I could go home the next week!

Thursday, May 27, brought a visit from one of the most special men God ever planted on planet earth. His name is Charles Martin. Just prior to our coming to Tecumseh, Charles was the Tecumseh city manager and he and his family were faithful members of First Baptist Church. He left Tecumseh and took a position in Fredrick, Oklahoma. Fredrick is just about as far south as you can go in the state without getting your feet wet in the Red River. I got to know the Martins when they returned for visits to Tecumseh.

By 2020, Charles was retired and living in Altus, Oklahoma, about ninety miles southwest of Anadarko. Thursday afternoon Charles made a surprise visit. Charles stands about six foot, six inches tall. He played quarterback in his day at Iowa State University. Well into his eighties, Charles still is an imposing figure. He is a devout man of God and has the gift of encouragement.

A few years before his visit to the hospital, Charles had visited our church. On a yellow guest card Charles had written this message which was later passed on to me. The message read, "Tony, you are doing a great job. Thanks for loving God and loving people." I cherished that card so much I stored it away in my Bible.

After we chatted for a few minutes, I pulled out that yellow card, passed it to Charles, and asked him if he remembered writing that message of encouragement to me. He didn't. Some may chalk that up to him being in his eighties. Maybe, but I like to think it was because Charles is so proficient at encouraging people that he can't remember all the times he has done so.

Chris, our exuberant and helpful nurse practitioner, came by on Friday, May 28, to tell us their biggest concern about releasing me was the condition of my bedsore wound. If Dr. Tu felt the healing had progressed enough, she would sign off to let me go home the next week.

I mentioned earlier we had received a window visit from Alicia's sister, Tracie, and fiance, Cody. On Saturday, May 29, Cody and Tracie would trade in their titles of fiance' and fiancée for the titles of husband and wife. They planned a simple but beautiful ceremony for that morning in the backyard of Tracie's home in Mustang. Tracie and I had been big buddies for several years. When I Alicia and I first started dating, Tracie was a ten-year-old with a Dorothy

Hamill haircut, a cute button nose, and a smile so warm it could melt the coldest stone.

I was teaching and coaching at Mustang High School then. During the football season the pep club would sell spirit ribbons on Fridays with a picture depicting what the Broncos were going to do to that week's opponent. The pep club sponsor was kind enough to sell me two ribbons on Thursdays. I would get them to Tracie so she and a friend could wear them to her elementary school on Fridays. Being the only kids with spirit ribbons that made them big girls on campus.

In had been her desire that I would perform her wedding when that special day happened. But my health condition at that time made officiating the wedding impossible. We settled for me offering an electronic closing prayer. David and Terri came to the hospital to be my tech team. They connected me with the wedding party and at the conclusion of the ceremony, I was able to offer the closing prayer of blessing for her and Cody.

Alicia told me later that during the prayer, a few tears were shed, but this time they were tears of joy. I cried tears of sorrow when I found out following the ceremony everyone feasted on barbecue. That was a summer bummer.

Alicia's brother, Buck, and his family drove up from Houston to Mustang for the festivities. On Saturday afternoon all of them drove down to Anadarko, along with Alicia, and I made another trip outside and visited with them. We enjoyed beautiful weather and an equally as beautiful visit. This taste of normalcy was bitter sweet. I was so happy to see them, but so sad that when everyone left because I couldn't go with them. My day of attending celebrations would one day happen, but that day wasn't May 28, 2021.

I had been experiencing some nausea in those days, and Saturday afternoon I had another bout with it. We had tried various treatments, but this time I was given a concoction called a Green Lizard Cocktail. It sounded suspect for something a Baptist preacher would be consuming. The ingredients of a Green Lizard Cocktail typically contain the antacids aluminum hydroxide, magnesium hydroxide, and calcium carbonate along with lidocaine. Sometimes an antispasmodic is thrown in for good measure. It was a jolt to swallow, but it was effective in killing the nausea.

How about another exciting holiday? Monday May 31 was Memorial Day. We celebrated by, well, pretty much doing what we did every day in the hospital. One day looked like another day which was highly similar to the day before that.

But days are what you make of them. Whether you are tight in the clutches of a long pandemic recovery, or just wading through life in general, you may not be able to control your circumstances, but you can have a say in how you respond to them.

The Old Testament book of Lamentations is pretty well as advertised, a book of laments of regrets, disappointments, and sorrows. It is offered by God's prophet, Jeremiah, and penned for the purpose of public grieving over the destruction of the city of Jerusalem, and the sacred Temple there. Lamentations was also a personal expression of Jeremiah's grief.

Jeremiah was a brother who had been through the ringer. He is considered a major prophet and experienced some major problems. God gave one sermon for Jeremiah, to stand on the street corners of Jerusalem and preach: "God will send a vicious conquering army from Babylon to wipe out this place, so you just as well surrender when they get here."

The sermon was simple, but highly unpopular with King Zedekiah and the citizens of Jerusalem. In the fall of 1983, singer Anne Murray released the song, "Sure Could Use a Little Good News" lamenting all the crime and sorrow in the culture. It was just as well Jeremiah wasn't around in 1983 because he would have no good news to offer Anne then either.

Jeremiah also had no good news for King Zedekiah. Zedekiah was guilty of searching for a source who would tell him what he wanted to hear. He employed several false prophets who claimed God would come swooping down to Jerusalem and to their rescue. But God told Jeremiah to make a wooden yoke for himself, wear it down main street, preaching that the Jews of Jerusalem were the oxen, and Babylon would be their heavy yoke. Hananiah, one of the phony baloney prophets, took the yoke from Jeremiah and told the people God would intervene for them within two years and crush Babylon for them. Sounded good. It just wasn't true.

But Jeremiah persisted in preaching the truth from God and for his honorarium for preaching he was beaten and placed in stocks, received a death sentence from the priests and false prophets, had his sermon notes cut to shreds and burned, was cast into an empty cistern and left to die there in the mud, and was publicly labeled a liar. Ain't ministry fun.

As in turned out, God and Jeremiah knew what they were talking about. The Babylonian army invaded Jerusalem around 597 B.C. They took most of the people as captives including the king who had his eyes gouged out and was forced to march back to Babylon.

This was Jeremiah's world. Does it sound something like the pitiful predicament you find yourself in now? If you aren't sure, compare your sufferings with what Jeremiah enumerated in Lamentations 3:1-20 (NIV).

> "I am the man who has seen affliction by the rod of the Lord's wrath. 2 He
>
> has driven me away and made me walk in darkness rather than light; 3
>
> indeed, he has turned his hand against me again and again, all day long.
>
> 4 He has made my skin and my flesh grow old and has broken my bones.
>
> 5 He has besieged me and surrounded me with bitterness and hardship.
>
> 6 He has made me dwell in darkness like those long dead. 7 He has walled
>
> me in so I cannot escape; he has weighed me down with chains. 8 Even
>
> when I call out or cry for help, he shuts out my prayer. 9 He has
>
> barred my way with blocks of stone; he has made my paths crooked.

10 Like a bear lying in wait, like a lion in hiding, 11 he dragged me from the

path and mangled me and left me without help. 12 He drew his bow and

made me the target for his arrows. 13 He pierced my heart with arrows

from his quiver. 14 I became the laughingstock of all my people; they mock

me in song all day long. 15 He has filled me with bitter herbs and given me gall to drink. 16 He

has broken my teeth with gravel; he has trampled me in the dust.

17 I have been deprived of peace; I have forgotten what prosperity is.

18 So I say, "My splendor is gone and all that I had hoped from the

Lord." 19 I remember my affliction and my wandering, the bitterness

and the gall. 20 I well remember them, and my soul is downcast within me.

Wow! Now, that is a major league lament. Maybe you are suffering from similar sorrow and feel you are being treated in a similar way as Jeremiah was. Life can beat you down to the point that you begin to doubt if the God who created you, "fearfully and wonderfully" as David proclaimed in Psalm 139, even knows what is going on in your life.

You may be thinking, "Thank you, Tony, for the pep talk. I think I'll take all this encouragement and go jump off a bridge."

But don't do that yet. I've spent the previous seven paragraphs and twenty verses of scripture just to show you the conclusion Jeremiah came to beginning in the next verse, verse 21.

Jeremiah 3:21-23 (NIV), "²¹ Yet this I call to mind and therefore I have hope: ²² Because of the Lord's great love we are not consumed, for his compassions never fail. ²³ They are new every morning; great is your faithfulness."

Talk about a spiritual and emotional 180! Even with all that Jeremiah had been through and in the midst of a mental meltdown, he couldn't give up on God, because God never gave up on him. Before Jeremiah gave up on himself and sold out on God, he circled back to his faith. He would spend from verses 22 through 66 singing the praises of God for his mercy and provisions.

If you have a Bible and it has Jeremiah Chapter 3 in it, invest the time to read what truly is a message of encouragement for hurting hearts and struggling souls.

Before you bail out on God because you believe He has bailed out on you, walk through those verses from Jeremiah's pen that God preserved for you so that you may use them as you try to keep your ship with the sail up and the keel down in the midst of your personal storm. Is there anything in that passage that isn't true? Jeremiah's words of hope inspired Thomas Chisholm to compose these encouraging lyrics.

> Great is Thy faithfulness, O God my Father
> There is no shadow of turning with Thee
> Thou changest not, Thy compassions, they fail not
> As Thou hast been, Thou forever will be
>
> Great is Thy faithfulness
> Great is Thy faithfulness
> Morning by morning new mercies I see
> All I have needed Thy hand hath provided
> Great is Thy faithfulness, Lord, unto me
>
> (Chisholm, Thomas and William M. Runyan, 1923, "Great Is Thy Faithfulness" bibliography info)

Let me invite you to author your own book of Lamentations in this fashion. First, get something to eat if you are hungry, then make the time to get a good night's rest. Hunger and fatigue led the great prophet Elijah to run like a scared rabbit from the threats of Queen Jezebel. Then take pen and paper and write out your current list of lamentations to God. Be specific about what situations are plaguing you. Then do a Jeremiah 180 and list at least five occasions when God has provided for you through previous storms.

Read it all to God in the form of a personal prayer, a private conversation in which you have the sympathetic ear of the Creator of the Universe. Save it for the day when God salvages your train wreck and makes something good from it. Then celebrate the victory God has given you!

On the one-year anniversary of entering SSM Hospital in Shawnee, Alicia and I traveled up to the third floor of SSM to the waiting room area of the Intensive Care Unit where three times I grasped the knob on death's doorway only to be pulled back by the hand of God.

We found a private place and read scriptures that we had chosen earlier in the day. My selection was Psalm 46:1-4. Alicia read from 1 Peter 5:10-11 which was a passage recommended to her by her good friend, Terri. Then, on my phone, I played a song given to Alicia as encouragement by multiple friends at multiple times. The song was "Through It All" by Andrea Crouch. The first verse and chorus set the tone for the moving message of the song.

> I've had many tears and sorrows,
> I've had questions for tomorrow,
> There's been times I didn't know right from wrong.
> But in every situation,
> God gave me blessed consolation,
> that my trials come to only make me strong.
>
> Through it all,
> through it all,
>
> I've learned to trust in Jesus,
> I've learned to trust in God.
>
> Through it all,
> through it all,
> I've learned to depend upon His Word.

We concluded our visit with a prayer of praise and thanksgiving.

Before we left the ICU area, Alicia took a picture of me, standing strong and tall (well, relatively strong compared to what I was the year before) under scripture written on the outside wall of the ICU which read, "For with God nothing shall be impossible." Luke 1:37.

After a celebratory meal in Shawnee, we returned home and for the first time, Alicia read to me her laments from her first journal of our journey covering the time I was in SSM. And, yep, I cried. I cried big old tears of joy and gratitude.

***God is great, and I'm so grateful for His infinite mercies!***

# THERE'S NO PLACE LIKE HOME

# CHAPTER 22 - "The Surreal Deal"

## The Encouragement of Answered Prayer

We were still negotiating with my toes on the issue of getting my shoes and AFO braces on without the toes bending underneath my feet. Physical Therapist Justin came to my room on Wednesday, June 2, and taped my big toe and the adjacent toe together on my left foot. I'm not sure what the second toe is called. Maybe "not quite so big" toe. Those two toes were the biggest culprits to bending, but with the tape job, they stood together fairly well.

Chris, the PA, delivered the news that x-rays on my lungs were clear and they were showing signs of improving. Goodbye, pneumonia!

With the promise of going home looking more like a reality, we had to decide what would be the best mode of transportation for the trip whether it would be a transporter, similar to an ambulance but not as heavily stocked with equipment, or in Alicia's SUV. We decided to take a field trip that afternoon around Anadarko in her SUV to determine how I might respond to a longer trip back home in that fashion.

For my part, the results seemed inconclusive. I tolerated the trip around town well, but I had concerns about what we would do if something went wrong on the longer trip home. We took the safe route and opted for the transport.

Thursday, June 3, had the potential to be one of the most important days on our journey up to this point. Dr. Tu would come by for wound care, then she would decide if the wound healing had progressed to a point that I could be released.

*Thursday, June 3*

**HOME TOMORROW 9 AM!**

That brief entry said it all. After a 193-day journey through five hospitals, I would be going home. The thought of it choked me up then and still does now.

As I looked back at the agonizing days Alicia and I had endured over the six and a half months in hospitals, I couldn't conceive this day ever arriving. As tightly as I tried to wrap it, it was difficult to wrap my head around the idea that tomorrow I would be on my way to our little log house outside of Tecumseh.

The reality of the moment set in at sunrise on Friday morning, June 4. This would be our personal Victory Day.

When I arrived in Anadarko back in April for what we hoped would be my last stop before being released, I had the idea that I would rehab to the point I could walk unassisted, one morning pack up my belongings, and stroll down the hallway of the hospital, out the door, and head for home.

But it didn't work that way. The hospital staff wants to get a patient to the point of dismissal almost as much as the patient does. But that means a complete recovery wasn't the goal. The goal was to see me progress to the point I could go home and continue my rehab using the services of home health nurses and physical and occupational therapists. Before being dismissed, I would need to be able to eat solid food and perform some basic tasks; chief among them would be to be able to transfer myself from the bed to a walker in order to go the short distances I needed for daily living.

When the transporter crew came for me, I was given the option of walking out or riding on a gurney. Walking was my preference; but at that time, the distance I would have to walk would require at least one rest stop and as much as five minutes to recoup before moving on. That would be very time consuming for everyone; so reluctantly, I took the ride out of the hospital on a gurney.

As I mentioned earlier, we had great experiences with hospital staff wherever we went, but there were those that seem to stand out. At Anadarko, one of those for Alicia and I was Nurse Jessica. She went above and beyond for us in our stay at Anadarko, and we would miss her.

She came into my room just before time to leave and we shared a tearful goodbye and would repeat it just before being loaded into the transport. Thank you, Lord, for special people you place in our lives.

As I was wheeled out of Room 210, I was greeted with

cheers by members of the hospital staff gathered at the nurses' station. A similar reception occurred as I exited the hospital. How crazy were the emotions that struggled with each other when I desperately wanted to go home yet would miss these wonderful people.

But I don't think Alicia was on board with any idea of bringing them home with us.

At 9:30 a.m., we began the final leg in God's miraculous efforts to beat Covid and return home. Tracie and Cody hooked up our travel trailer at Longview Church, Alicia's home away from home since April 20, and hauled it back to Tecumseh for us.

Traveling home I got a call from Alicia. She said a group from our church and the community would be gathered near Tecumseh's one and only traffic light to welcome us when we came through town. One difference between a transporter and an ambulance is the transporter has side windows in the rear portion. Alicia wanted me to be certain to look out the windows when we drove through town.

A series of calls followed with Alicia telling me she had been contacted by two Oklahoma City television stations wanting to interview us when we arrived home. Due to the deadlines for each reporter to do the interview and get back to Oklahoma City, both reporters would have to meet at our home at the same time.

It seemed a bit awkward to us; but both reporters, Barry Mangold and Katelyn Ogle, had worked together at the same television station before, so they were both good with meeting at the same time.

As promised, when we drove through Tecumseh, there was a group of town folk waiting with signs and balloons welcoming us. A bonus surprise was that among the crowd were Kaitlyn and our three grandchildren, Jordy, Jaybea, and Johnny holding signs reading "Welcome Home, Bud!" (Bud is the name the grandchildren call me by because I wanted us to be big buddies).

The caravan of the transport, Alicia in the SUV, and Cody Layman pulling our travel trailer all arrived at our house together, safe and sound. My base of operation in our home would be a rented hospital bed in the front room. Micah Sanchez from Tecumseh Oxygen and Medical Supply was at the house still setting up the hospital bed. So, I landed in the recliner from which I had slipped out of and onto the floor 193 days ago.

Barry and Katelyn set up their lights and cameras and conducted their interviews.

Both were gracious and put together great reports shown that night on their respective stations, News Nine KWTV and Channel Four, KFOR. Later in the summer we got a visit from Craig Whitney, a former member of our youth group, who told me, "You sure paid a heavy price for your fifteen minutes of fame!"

If this experience was about gaining notoriety, I should have had my head examined!

In time, the reporters, family members, and friends left, and it was just Alicia and I in our own little home. Using the name of a sketch from the Carol Burnett Show, I had in the past referred to us as "Old Folks at Home." Alicia detested that, so I let that comment slide this time.

We were finally home, and things were headed in a great direction. That was until we decided to use my walker to get me from the recliner to the hospital bed.

As I took hold of the walker handles and began to push upward, I discovered two significant things. My recliner was a rocker recliner, so when I pushed down, it went down. Also, our entire home has tile flooring. I was wearing only socks on my feet, so the downward motion of the recliner and my sliding on the tile resulted in me landing in a crumpled pile on the living room floor. Victories can be short lived.

In my entire hospital stay I had never been on the floor, something for which I was extremely grateful. The level of my physical progress did not give me confidence that I could do much to break a fall. Fortunately, this mishap wasn't a fall. There was no heavy impact as I went down. It went like I was sliding into home plate. Nevertheless there I was in the floor and Alicia, and I couldn't get me off of it.

Alicia called for help from David Williams. Soon he arrived, and I found it difficult to nonchalantly greet a house guest while lying on the living room floor. "Hey, David! So good of you to drop by." But this wasn't about being a good host. It was about getting upright.

The two of them struggled mightily but finally got me seated on a small stool. From there, they could get their arms underneath my arms to create enough leverage to get me vertical and over to my bed.

As the afternoon wound down, and reality was trying its best to sink in, I had a surreal moment. In Murray County, Oklahoma, it might be pronounced, "It's sure real!" But surreal isn't about being real. It is used to describe something bizarre, weird, a dream or fantasy.

My surreal moment occurred as I began to look around our home. We have an open floor plan which allowed me to see our kitchen and dining room from the living room where I reclined on my very own rented hospital bed. From that lofty position, I saw the kitchen island where around which I used to chase our grandchildren. I saw the refrigerator door art gallery displaying pictures drawn by our grandchildren, held in place by decorative magnets acquired as souvenirs on family vacations.

High on a wall, I saw a mount of a buck deer I took on a hunting trip to Medford, Oklahoma, years before. I saw a long, three shelf cabinet on the back wall of our dining room containing nick after knack including my mother's old butter churn I used to crank by hand when I was a boy. On the same wall I saw a large picture depicting the Lord's Supper where Jesus and the twelve apostles looked down upon us whenever we ate our own supper at the dining room table. I saw a small shelf on another wall holding about two dozen country church collector pieces, each given, one by one, to Alicia by Terri each Christmas. I saw the sixty-inch television with which we had indulged ourselves on my sixty-fourth birthday. And finally, I saw a sign above our front door that reads "WITH GOD ALL THINGS ARE POSSIBLE." Truer words were never written. I had exited under that sign as a very sick man and had reentered a healthier man 193 days later.

The whole thing was so familiar, yet so surreal (there's that word again). I knew this place by heart. It was home. But it took every piece of gray matter I had to convince myself I was finally here. Painful days and sleepless nights in multiple hospitals had convinced me that what I was experiencing now would never occur.

But if you pray for something, expect to receive it. James, the half-brother of Christ and the full believer in Christ, tells us in James 1:6-8 (NIV),

> "**⁶ But when you ask, you must believe and not doubt, because the**
>
> **one who doubts is like a wave of the sea, blown and tossed by the**
>
> **wind. ⁷ That person should not expect to receive anything from the**
>
> **Lord. ⁸ Such a person is double-minded and unstable in all they do.**"

No one wants to be described as being double-minded any more than one wants to be described as being two-faced. But a quandary can occur in the mind of a believer when he reads from scripture, "Ask and you will receive", "You have not because you ask not", or "Whatever you ask in my name, I will do it."

I had prayed a bushel basket full of times for God to just get me back home. And He did. It wasn't an overnight event, except on June 3, 2021. But it eventually happened.

Yet I have prayed for things with equal the enthusiasm as I prayed to come home, yet those things never came to be. Were they not answered because I didn't pray in faith? Well, if we are to believe James 1:6, and I believe we should, yes, a prayer offered in weak faith gets a disappointing answer.

But don't believe that every prayer offered that doesn't see the desired answer is always due to a lack of faith. So, if prayers offered in weak faith may not give the desired answer, and prayers offered in strong faith still may not give the desired answer, why pray? Because praying is a large and vital part of our job as believers. Believers pray.

You may understand what God is doing with your prayers, or you may never know what God is doing with your prayers; but that doesn't change what we must do. Pray.

Let's listen in again on the prayer of Jesus, the very Son of God, which He lifted to His Father in the Garden of Gethsemane.

Among other places in the Gospels, we find the prayer of Jesus that night. Mark 14: 36 (CSB) says, "And he said, 'Abba, Father! All things are possible for you. Take this cup away from me.'"

Did His Father take away the cup? Did Jesus escape hanging on a cross to take upon Himself every sin of the world, past, present and future? Did He miss out on having to endure the holy wrath of His Father? The short answer is "No."

How can we not believe the prayer of Jesus was a prayer of faith? The words of Jesus just prior to His prayer in Mark 14:34 (CSB) seem to indicate proper motivation for such. "[33] He took Peter, James, and John with him, and he began to be deeply distressed and troubled. [34] He said to them, 'I am deeply grieved to the point of death. Remain here and stay awake.'" That indicates a deep motivation and a relentless faith.

And while we are in Mark 14, let's look at the last sentence

Tony Peake   199

in Jesus' prayer found in verse 36. "Nevertheless not what I will, but what you will." Now don't think for a moment that Jesus was hedging His bet or that He was providing an excuse for God should He not take away the cup of the crucifixion. God doesn't need for us to provide Him an escape route.

Jesus petitioned God with a solid prayer of faith. And God's answer was, "I'm sorry, but there is no other way to save the lost souls of mankind. You must drink the cup."

Visiting with family and friends after returning home, I heard many times, "Prayer works." I knew exactly what they meant and agreed with the sentiment. But we must realize that when it comes to prayer, God works. Prayer is just the avenue offered to us to request what we desire for Him to do, and we must do so in faith that God will work in His own divine way.

Recently, I drove by SSM Hospital in Shawnee and looked up to the third-floor windows of the ICU room where my soul was almost launched into eternity several times. If I wanted to ask God a "why" question, that question might be, "Why did you spare me?" There was, and still is, nothing about me that would merit God sparing me from drinking that cup. But he did. And all I can do is believe there is a reason and pray I don't miss perceiving what that reason is so that I might fulfill the purpose He has for me.

There it is. I experienced the surreal moment of finally experiencing my answered prayers to come back home; and if you live the life of faithful prayer, you will experience surreal moments as well. Give God thanks, no matter in what way He answers, and keep faithfully walking toward that ultimate trip home to glory.

*God is great, and I am grateful for the surreal moments of answered prayers!*

# CHAPTER 23

# The Pathway to Victory

*The Value of Trusting God*

On the day I arrived home, reporter Barry Mangold asked me what I might tell someone going through difficulties of the magnitude I did. My answer to that question has evolved to four points of encouragement.

## 1. TRUST IN GOD

You are going to trust in someone or something even if you believe that no one can be trusted. That becomes your belief system.

So I recommend you put your trust in the One who "determines the number of stars and calls them each by name (Psalm 147:4 NIV). The reason God can call the stars by name is because He created each one and named each one. That sounds like a good place to put your trust.

## 2. DON'T GIVE UP

Joshua 14: 6 (NIV), "Haven't I told you, be strong and courageous. That sounds like a no-brainer, but it is vital to regularly remind yourself, "No matter what happens, I'm not going to give up." In my younger (and dumber) days, I thought I was a bull rider. As a rider sits down on the back of the bull in the chute, a buddy will be standing on the chute gate to pull the slack out of the rider's bull rope so that he may tightly wrap the tail of the rope around his hand. In essence, he is locking himself aboard the fifteen hundred pounds of angry hamburger meat on which he sits (I told you it is dumb).

As the rider nods for the crew to open the chute gate, he will often hear his buddy yell, "Don't forget to try!" That is a no-brainer, too, but it is always encouraging to hear that reminder.

In your battle to overcome whatever challenge is pummeling you, it is essential you keep yelling to your spirit, "Don't forget to try!"

Someone said that in martial arts a black belt is just a white belt that wouldn't give up. There may be times you get discouraged, depressed, and you may need to shed some big tears; just don't give up. One of my physical therapist told me about a patient who had progressed to the point he made the triumphant walk down the same 150-foot hallway in Anadarko that I did. The therapists celebrated his accomplishment with him, returned him to his bed, and he refused to ever get out of it again. Eventually, one day an ambulance pulled up to the hospital and hauled him away to a nursing home, likely where he would spend the rest of his life.

Lest I be judgmental about a situation in which I don't know all the circumstances, perhaps the patient had good reason to stay in bed. But if that would be his decision, it is important that the reason be valid and compelling. Heed the advice of that great theologian, John Wayne, "You may make a lot of mistakes, but don't let quitting be one of them."

## 3. BE PATIENT

Early on in my stay in ICU at Select Hospital, the physical therapists came in one day to evaluate what I was able to do. First, the team had to lift me up in the bed because I was unable to do that myself. Second, they had to swing my legs over the side to sit me on the edge of the bed for the evaluation. After that, it was necessary for a PT to be in front of me and one behind me to hold me upright so I would not to fall out on the floor.

With that accomplished they continued to tell me, "Tony, lift up your head. Lift up your head." Who can't lift their own head? For a long time, me. Then I was requested to perform certain tasks – make a fist (I couldn't), lift my arm (I did partially), and several other tasks (which I did poorly).

Finally and mercifully, they laid me back in bed. After they exited my room, I closed my eyes and thought, "You think you are going to walk again? You can't even sit up in the bed by yourself!"

Eventually, I did walk again. But it was a long, arduous trip from where I was then. If I hadn't found the ability to be patient and let the process slowly play out day by day, I would have grown discouraged and would never walk as I do now.

During my first office visit with Dr. Tony Haddad after I returned home, he told me to measure my progress by months, not days. If I measured progress day by day, I wouldn't notice any progress and grow discouraged.

Rome wasn't built in a day. And for me, my Covid wasn't defeated in a day. Likely, if your trials are of any significance, you will not see them resolved in a day. Be patient.

## 4. CELEBRATE THE VICTORIES

I don't care how small your victories; celebrate them. Recognizing progress and celebrating can encourage you to keep going and keep accepting new challenges.

Seeing my physical therapist arrive each day brought a sense of dread. I never knew what new exercise they would drag me through. Some would sound impossible for me. But I experienced success by deciding, "Okay, I will try this. It probably won't be pretty. I may fail miserably, but I will never accomplish it until I first give it a try."

This mindset would carry me through chores like standing beside my bed holding on to my walker for as long as I possibly could, pushing myself to take those first meager eight steps, stretching myself to walk farther down the hallway than the day before.

My home health care physical therapist, Sheila Powell, told me at the end of one of her visits one day that next time she came we would stand up by my bed without holding on to any support. A few days later the goal was to walk by using my walker up the hillside from my house to our detached garage on our gravel driveway.

In time we would stretch out the walks to go the forty yards to my mailbox. How about walking with just using a cane, taking on the nine-step stairway from our back door to the garage, strolling cane in hand around the perimeter of our spacious yard? Each one of those accomplishments were preceded by celebrations of previous events.

Megan Radunzel, my outpatient physical therapist, would have me push a wooden bridge with 120 pounds, across the PT room four times. She would have me lifting weights, walking across the room while restrained by a bungee cord. She would eventually have me lie down on my back on a pad and attempt to get on my feet without holding onto anything for support.

In time I was able to complete every one of those tasks. But the first time I tried each one, the results were ugly. They continued to be ugly for a while until I could master them. But I learned to celebrate every tiny bit of progress, even if the progress was simply that I gave each one a try.

That was the secret. Whatever I was asked to do, my job was to make that initial effort. And I had my own little victory party in my head, no matter how small the results.

Don't short sell your dreams just yet. Before David was a king, he was a meager shepherd boy. Before Moses was the leader of the exodus of God's people from Egypt, he was tending the herds of his father-in-law, Jethro, out there a hundred miles beyond nowhere. Before Mary was the mother of our Savior, she was an adolescent girl most likely focused on her friends and one day meeting Mr. Right. Before the mustard seed became a plant sturdy enough to be able to bear a bird's nest, it was, well, a mustard seed. Dream your dreams and celebrate each step along the way.

That's the way. Decide what is the next step you need to take. Prepare for it as best you can. Take the step. Celebrate any and all results. Use them as a springboard for more successes.

What is your big challenge now? Where can you get assistance on how to overcome it? What should be your first step? Will you give up or give up on giving up? And will you trust God, the God from whom all blessings flow? You bet your ever-loving champion mindset you will!

***God is great, and I'm grateful for every victory He gives me!***

# CHAPTER 24

# Down the Home Stretch

The Encouragement of Finishing

Coming home didn't signify the end. It was merely the end of the hospital recuperation phase and the beginning of the home recuperation phase.

I would like to take you on a whirlwind tour of some of the highlights of the next nine months after returning home in the ongoing journey toward recuperation.

JUNE 2021

Wednesday, June 9

Nurse Connie Kellner came from home health care for her first of four months of visits. It was a challenge for her to learn the process of changing out the dressing on my wound as Dr. Tu wanted it done, but she never backed down from the challenge.

Friday, June 11

About 11 p.m. I called out to Alicia for help. I was struggling to breathe. She eventually called 911 for an ambulance. This scared Alicia on two levels. First, she obviously was concerned about my condition. Second, she would tell me later that she believed this would be our life from now on, me struggling to breathe and ambulances taking me to the emergency room. But with some steroids and breathing treatments that night, I recovered well and was sent home. We arrived back home at 3 a.m. and unloaded in a driving rain. Thank God I haven't been back to an emergency room since that night.

Tuesday, June 15

We made our first visit for outpatient care with Dr. Tu in Stroud, Oklahoma.

In those days, my bedsore wound pain really became a pain, pun greatly intended. It would be several weeks before I could lie comfortably on my back.

Wednesday, June 16

We made my first visit to pulmonologist, Dr. Tony Haddad. It was on this visit Dr. Haddad told me that (medically speaking) I had no reason to be alive, but praise God, I was.

Soon after returning home I was contemplating my future recovery. It dawned on me that no doctor, nurse, or physical therapist had ever told me that I would be able to walk unassisted again.

Dr. Tony assured me that I would get better, but I currently was only at the forty-yard line. With pauses to fight back tears (surprise, surprise) I told him that was okay. I just wanted to know if there were any of the field left in front of me to improve.

Saturday, June 19

Saturday afternoon began with me receiving the best Father's Day gift I believe I've ever had. I had not been able to see any of our grandchildren play baseball that summer and had made peace with the fact that I probably wouldn't.

Kaitlyn called to tell us Jordy was playing in a tournament that Saturday in Dale, Oklahoma, a thirty-minute trip from our home! We were able view the game sitting in lawn chairs under a shade tree in the nearby parking lot. After their first game and first win, Jordy's head coach, Bubba Mobbs, gave him a baseball to present to me. Jordy and all his teammates came to us in the parking lot and with a semi-toothless grin from ear to ear, Jordy handed me the ball. Then it was fist bumps with all the team. That ball now rests in its own clear plastic display case in our living room.

Jordy's team, The Southeast Elite, won both games that day. Father's Day gift number two. A great couple in our community, Randy and Suzanne Gilbert, have a daughter, Dusti, who is married to Jordan Baker, a major league umpire. Suzanne and family were there to watch her grandson and Jordan's son play. I was able to meet Jordan and have a picture taken with him.

The next afternoon, we traveled back to Dale to see The Southeast Elite win the tournament. Jordy was the tournament MVP for his age group, and he won the homerun contest. What a Father's Day! (I'm recuperating from Covid, but I am a helpless victim of pride in my grandchildren).

Thursday, June 24

We had an appointment in Oklahoma City with Dr. Bentley Edmonds, an orthopedic surgeon specializing in foot and ankle problems. We wanted to get his opinion on my toes that had turned under. He said he would not do anything immediately because it was possible for the foot to make that correction on its own. He recommended a special pair of running shoes to help with my foot problems. We bought the shoes, and in time the toes did improve.

## JULY 2021

Sunday, July 18

Our church was ordaining three new young deacons and our youth minister that evening. I was asked, if I thought I was able, to preach the sermon known as "The Charge" at the ordination service.

That evening Alicia and I arrived, and I made the trip inside in a wheelchair due to the distance required to make it to the front of the sanctuary would exceed the stamina of my walker and me. It was the first time I had been back in the church that I had served in for twenty-seven years since November 16, 2020, a length of 240 days. It was beyond thrilling to see all the church members and be able to preach. It was another one of those surreal moments.

A wonderful church member, Dr. Bob Evans, wrote this text following the service.

"Tonight I was able to see another Kirk Gibson moment (Kirk Gibson came off the bench in Game 1 of the 1988 World Series to hit a walk-off homerun despite the fact he had a leg injury that prevented him from walking normally, much less running normally. I am sure when he hit his homerun on one leg, he just swung hard and let it happen.). Tonight when Tony preached, he sounded like he had turned it over to God and swung for the fence, and it hasn't come down yet."

Tuesday, July 27

With all the enthusiasm of our forefathers when they won their independence from England, Alicia and I celebrated being taken off the wound vac. Free at last!

## AUGUST 2021

Sunday, August 1

Most of you will remember the date and the memories of your high school or college graduation, your wedding, the births of your children, buying your first home, and other special events in your lives. As for me, I will never forget the date, Sunday, August 1, 2021. On that day I resumed my duties as pastor and preached my first Sunday morning service sermon.

I shared some of the struggles and victories Alicia and I traveled through since falling out of my pulpit 256 days prior. The sermon was entitled "God Is Great and I Am Grateful" (If that doesn't sound familiar by now, you probably need to get back on your ADD meds). Nurse Andrea Jones from SSM Hospital in Shawnee, and husband attended the service!

While in the hospital I had two major goals: to preach again and to walk unassisted. One down, one to go.

Tuesday, August 17

I never thought I would be in a position to throw out the first pitch at a ballgame, but Alicia called me Monday afternoon saying Chad Trahan, Tecumseh High School fast pitch softball coach, asked me to throw out the first pitch at the team's first home game. I was thrilled, but big time nervous.

I always felt that if I ever were asked to throw out a first pitch, I wanted to do two things. One was to pitch the ball all the way from the pitching rubber, and the second was to not bounce the pitch on the way to home plate.

When Alicia came home from school, we went out into the front yard to practice the forty feet, underhanded style pitch. I was all over the place except home plate. Standing by the side of my walker, I was able to develop a pitching motion that had a modest chance of making all the way to home plate without bouncing.

Tuesday afternoon, I was introduced by the stadium announcer and received a warm welcome from the crowd.

My walker and I made our way to the pitching circle. I told the Tecumseh pitcher, Serenity Jacoway, I promised not to mess up her circle. For the most part, I didn't.

I've prayed some big-time prayers before. Let me pass the college exam, help me be a good husband, allow my children to be born healthy and grow up healthy, change the path of an oncoming tornado. But I prayed a big one standing on the pitching rubber. "Lord, please don't let me bounce it."

I stood in position, pulled the ball backward with my arm, swung forward, and let the ball fly in the afternoon sun. The pitch was high and outside, but catcher, Jessi Hull was able to corral it and run out to the pitching circle to give me the ball. All the girls on the softball team signed it for me.

# SEPTEMBER 2021

Friday, September 3

We attended the first Tecumseh High School football game. To climb the bleachers would be impossible; so Athletic Director, Jeff Shaffer, was gracious to allow us to come in the gate at the north end of the field and sit by the end zone.

By the football game on October 14, I would be able to climb the thirty steps of the stadium to take my usual seat on the top row. If there had been thirty-one steps, I don't think I would have made it.

Saturday, September 4

I took my first shower! Bathing up until this time consisted of me sitting in my wheelchair in the bathroom while Alicia and I co-oped a sponge bath. Today's version of a shower required I sit on a shower bench inside the tub. The shower didn't make me feel like a new man, but I did feel like a cleaner version of the old one.

Sunday, September 5

Another small step for man and a large step for recovery. I was able to lift my walker off the floor and walk. Those were my first solo steps in nine months!

Thursday, September 9

Nurse Connie did an exit evaluation. She would no longer be required to come change my bandage. Home health care physical therapy would also conclude at the end of September.

Sunday, September 12

I entered the church using only my cane. No more wheelchair. No more walker.

Thursday, September 16

One of my greatest dreams from my hospital days came true. I walked at home without the use of any type of aid!

Sunday, September 19

After church that evening, I had to pass Alicia's driving test by successfully driving my truck through our neighborhood. I did well enough that she asked me to drive her into town.

Monday, September 20

Since I was now mobile, I returned to the church office for the first time since falling ill with Covid. I was really enjoying all these "firsts."

Wednesday, September 22

During physical therapy, Sheila and I walked up the road on my old walking course I used for exercise prior to my illness. We made it all the way to the neighbor's sheep pasture which is about a 150-yard walk. That beat my 150-foot walk in the hospital in Anadarko by a mile! (Or at least by 100 yards). That stroll felt so wonderful.

Sunday, September 26

I preached the entire sermon while standing. At the end of the service, I introduced my guests, Nurse Connie Kellner and Physical Therapist Sheila Powell. As a surprise for Sheila and the congregation, I walked across the platform unassisted. What a thrill!

## OCTOBER 2021

Tuesday, October 12

I drove myself for the first time to my appointment with Dr. Tu. This would be my last. She released me from wound care. After 193 days in the hospital and 131 days back home, I was free from wound care. The wound area would continue to cause a measure of pain, but the wound was fully healed.

## NOVEMBER 2021

Wednesday and Thursday, November 3 and 4

I preached my first two funerals since returning, Delores Wilsie's on Wednesday, and Dot Stith's on Thursday. We rejoiced that two faithful women of God had received their heavenly rewards, but we grieved over the holes they left in our hearts.

Friday, November 25

We celebrated Thanksgiving with our family a day late. I had waited an entire year for turkey. I guess I could wait one more day.

I wrote a poem to read right before our meal and then planned to offer thanks to God, and oh, what thanks we had to offer.

Here is the poem I wrote for the occasion.

*"Thankful"*

*Gathered round this table*

*Are blessings young and old*

*As much as we are able*

*We thank You for each one*

*Thankful for our families*

*Thankful for this food*

*Thankful for this fellowship*

*That does our souls much good*

*Thankful for our health*

*Thankful for our jobs*

*Thankful for our wealth*

*You bless us gobs and gobs*

*Thankful for our country*

*Thankful for our schools*

*Thankful for each teacher*

*Who lives the Golden Rule*

*Thankful for our soldiers*

*Thankful we are free*

*Thankful for each day*

*That draws us close to Thee*

*But what we're thankful most for*

*That your Son paid the price*

*For us to be saved, saved, saved*

*By the blood of Jesus Christ*

*One last thing before I end*

*One last thing I'll say*

*This last year You pulled us through*

*To just be here today*

by Tony Peak, Thanksgiving 2021

As the time arrived to read the poem and offer the prayer, the lump in my throat and tears in my eyes made it impossible to do so. Instead Alicia did the reading and offered the prayer.

And then we ate turkey!

## DECEMBER 2021

Tuesday, November 30

As mentioned earlier, I had the privilege of speaking with two groups of nurses from SSM, some of which were taking such good care of me a year ago at this time.

Thursday, December 2

The Lord's Birthday!

We celebrated Christmas with our family and oh, how we celebrated. The weather was unseasonably warm, so the grandchildren were able to play outside with their new toys. What a wonderful day to celebrate the Giver of Life on a day I continued to celebrate the gift of my life and another Christmas with family.

## JANUARY AND FEBRUARY 2022

Thursday, January 6, 2022

I actually was alive and coherent for my birthday. My day was blessed by over 250 posts, texts, and cards wishing me a happy birthday.

Tuesday, February 1

I traveled to Oklahoma City at the recommendation of Megan Radunzel, my out care physical therapist, for an EMG test (Electromyography) with a neurologist. An EMG test involves shocking muscles to determine the health of the muscles.

The EMG revealed I had some irreversible damage in my lower legs. This would mean I would have my AFO braces perhaps the rest of my life. I was okay with that because, at least, I could walk.

Monday, February 14

After a great Valentine's Day meal at Paul's Steak House in Shawnee, Alicia and I returned home to continue a conversation we had been having for several weeks.

We believed it was time for us to end our ministry at First Baptist Church, Tecumseh, believing God was moving us in some new direction.

Sunday, February 20

At the conclusion of the morning service I read my letter of resignation. Following God's will is not always easy, and this was one of those times. We had invested twenty-seven years of our lives in the church and community. We had many good friends and many good memories in our time there.

I made my resignation effective Sunday, March 6.

## MARCH 2022

### Sunday, March 6

If we had to go out, what a blessed way to do so. I had been preaching a series of sermons from selected chapters of Psalms. My last Sunday was also the last Sunday of the series concluding with the last chapter of Psalms, Psalm 150.

The book of Psalms is rich with so many themes and topics. One of the foremost is wrestling with the idea that we have the love and protection of God in a world where we still experience so much pain and sorrows. But on this Sunday, we would do nothing but celebrate God.

We also praised the Lord by observing baptism. A boy named Drake Sanchez had given his life to Christ sometime earlier but wanted me to baptize him. It is always special to have the privilege of baptizing a new soul bound for heaven, but this one was extra-special in that I had baptized his mother when she was a member of our youth group when I was the youth minister. This would be my first baptism I was able to perform since returning from the hospital and it would be my last as pastor there.

Following the service we had a wonderful potluck dinner. I don't know about anyone else, but as for Baptists, if we meet, we eat. The members also blessed us with a money tree. I offered to give out free saplings from the tree after the dinner.

At the conclusion of the morning worship service, I addressed the congregation one last time. I remarked, "May these be the last words you here from me from this pulpit you have so graciously let me fill the past eleven years.

> "The LORD bless you
> and keep you;
> the LORD make his face shine on you
> and be gracious to you;
> the LORD turn his face toward you
> and give you peace.'"
>
> (Numbers 6:24-26 NIV)

And I leave you with those same words of blessing. It is my deepest desire that this book would bring glory to God and encouragement to you.

**God is great. *Be grateful.***

Engineer Pass. A plumper & healtier me, July 2020
(B.C. Before Covid)

Prayer Vigil at SSM Hospital Shawnee, OK.
December 8, 2020.

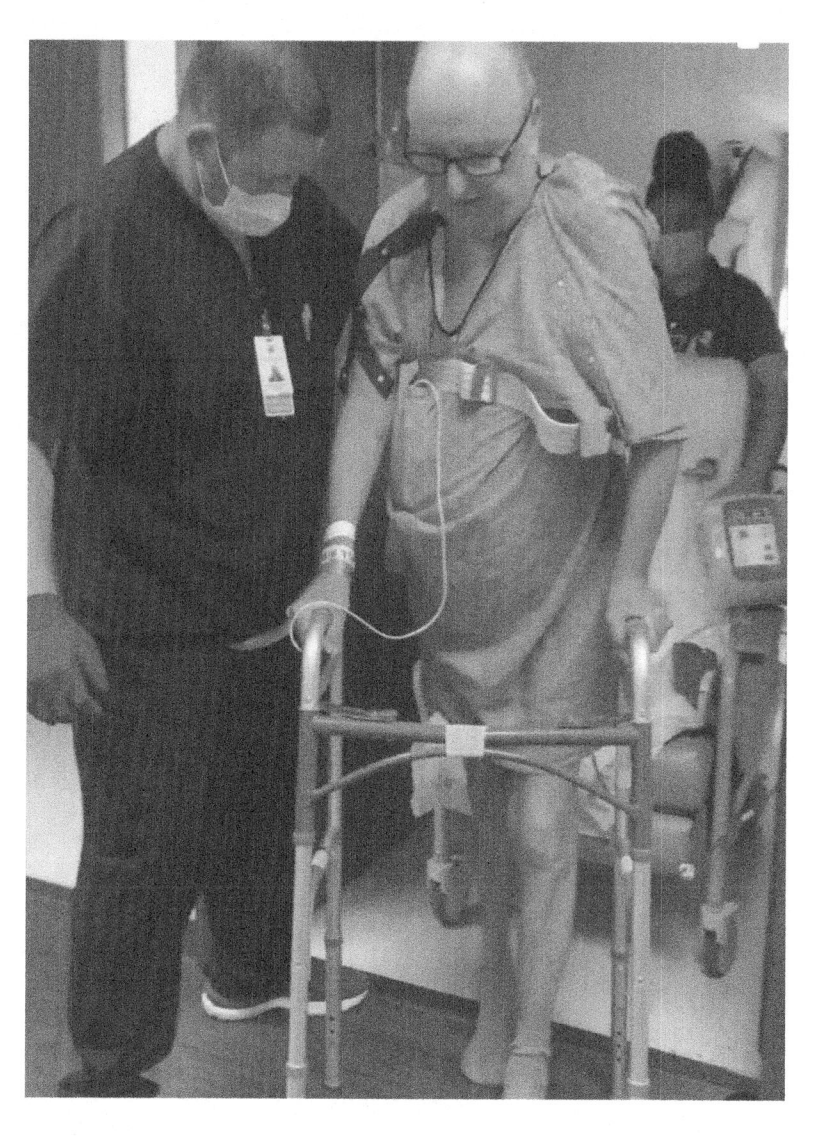

Early attempts at walking with PT Justin in Anadarko, May 2021.

**Reppin red for Bud!** 🤍

Caney basketball girls wearing red ribbons for me.
January 2021.

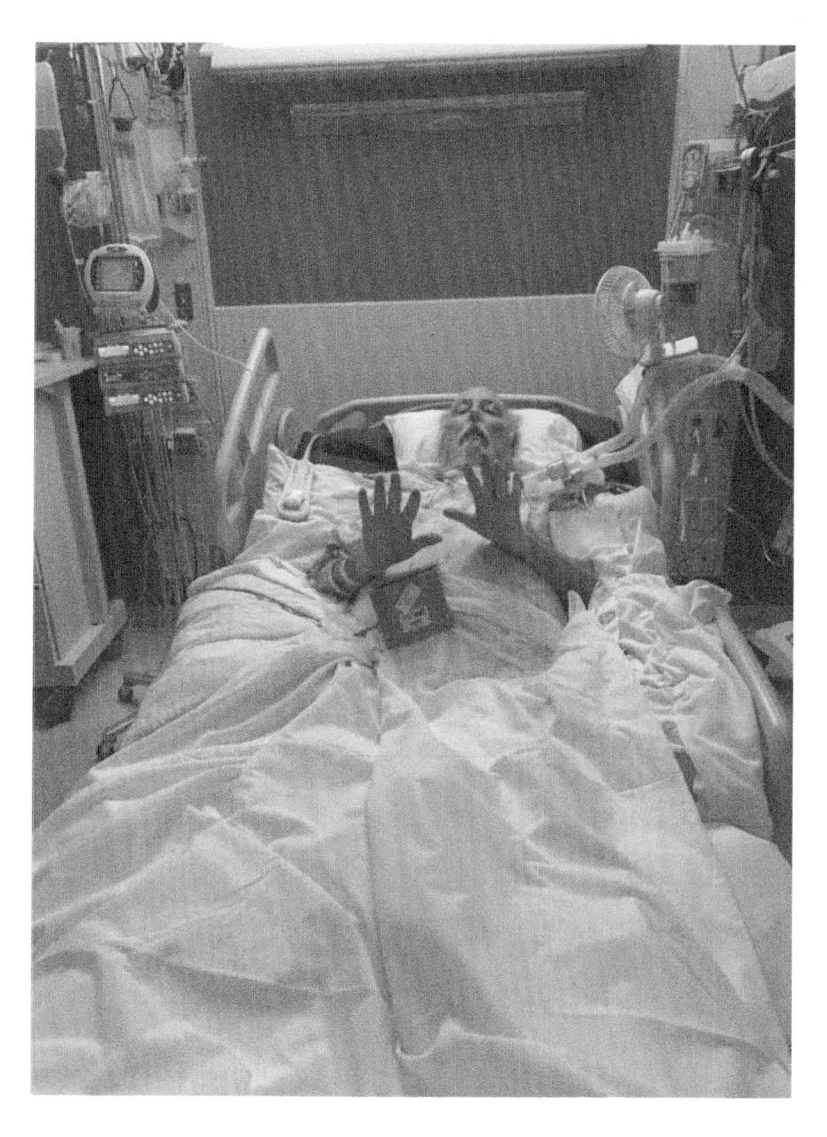

Select Hospital ICU in March 2021. First time
I was able to move my hands.

A visit from family May 2021 Anadarko.

228 God is Good and I am Grateful

Home Sweet Home with Alicia and the grandkids
June 2021.

First Sunday morning back to preach after
a 250 day absence, August 2021.

Jordy and his South East Elite team presented me with the game ball from their tournament win.
Father's Day June 2021.

Tony Peake  231

You're Out with Major League Umpire Jordan Baker at Father's Day tournament June 2021.

SSM Shawnee ICU waiting room on my one year anniversary of being hospitalized, November 2021.

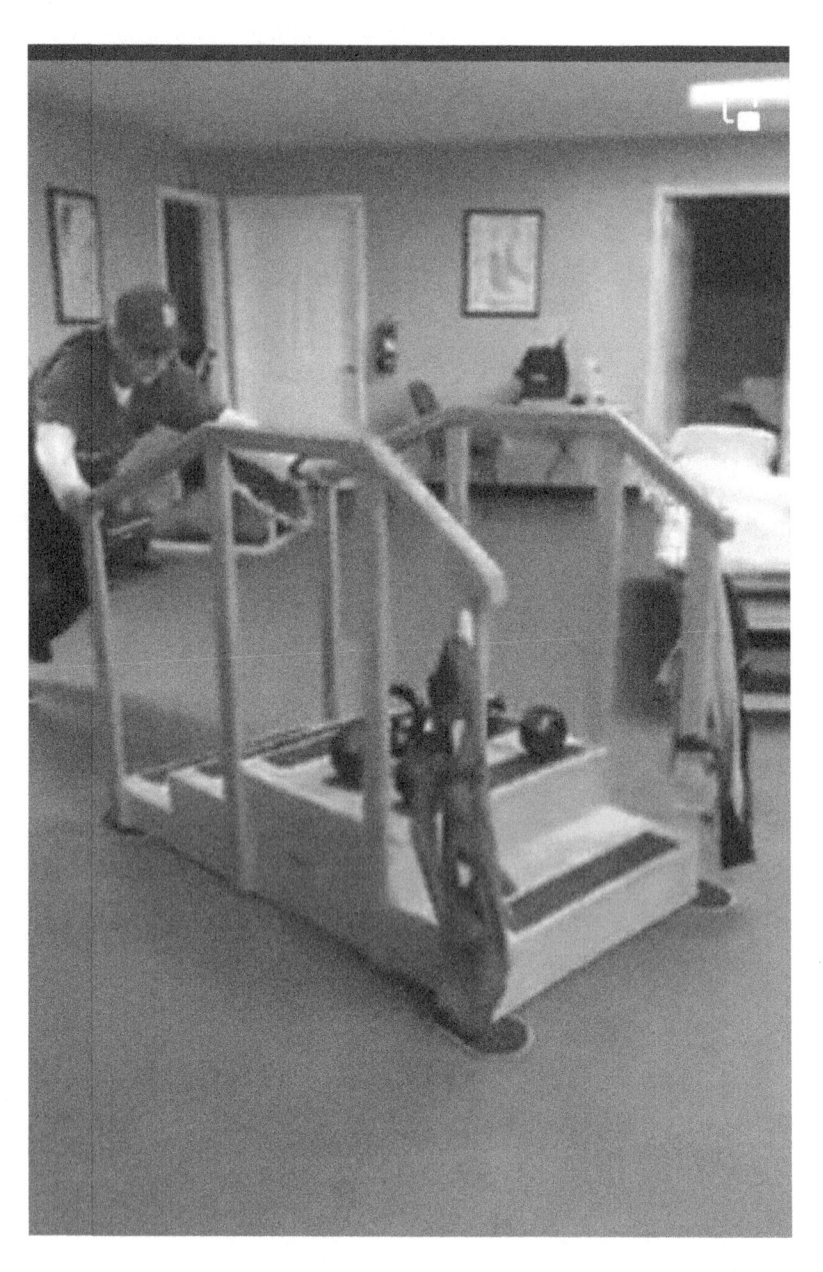

A little workout at Tecumseh Action Physical Therapy, February 2022.

Living the dream at Lake Irwin, Colorado.
September 2022.

# ACKNOWLEDGEMENTS

In a speech offered by Winston Churchill on the occasion of recognizing the bravery and valor of England's fighter pilots and bomber crews, he told his countrymen, "Never in the field of human conflict has so much been owed by so many to so few."

I amend the Prime Minister's words to say in my case, "Never have so few (Alicia and I) owed so much to so many. At the risk of leaving out some wonderful people, I will attempt to name individuals and groups which served us so well to get me healthy and get me home. Drawing from the notes in Alicia's journals and my own memory I am so grateful to the following.

I am grateful for Dr. Haddad, Dr. Anderson, Dr. Darvin, Dr. Brzozouski, Dr. Demaris, Dr. Cassaday, Nurse Lindsey, Nurse Kacy, Nurse Andrea, Nurse Danielle, Nurse Scott, Nurse Shanah, Nurse Sherri, Nurse Annie, Nurse Ashley, Nurse Lexi, Nurse Teresa, Nurse Ashley, Nurse Regina, Nurse Sabrina, Nurse Donna, Tech Mosha, Respiratory Therapist Nancy, Respiratory Therapist Tim, Nurse Todd, Nurse Bobbi, Nurse Moriah, and all the other wonderful staff members at SSM Hospital in Shawnee, Oklahoma.

I am grateful for Dr. Mohammed, Dr. Amed, Dr. Kahn,

Nurse Carrie, Nurse Sarah, Nurse Karen, Case Manager Beth, Nurse Zobia, Respiratory Therapist Karen, Nurse Nicoletta, Nurse Kristin, Nurse Simone, Nurse Andrew, Respiratory Therapist Jeremiah, Nurse Kristi, Nurse Nicole, Nurse Dominic, Nurse Michelina, Nurse Lauren, Nurse Lisa, Nurse Diane, Respiratory Therapist Todd, Respiratory Therapist Laura, Nurse Shelby, Respiratory Therapist Tiffany, Nurse Karmyn, Nurse Mondai, Respiratory Therapist Lisa, Nurse Katrina, Nurse Stacy, Physical Therapist Lisa, Respiratory Therapist Ron, Nurse Bobby, Nurse Jessica, Respiratory Therapist Becky, Nurse Caprice, Respiratory Therapist David, Nurse Theresa, Nurse Jody, Respiratory Therapist Ann, Case Manager Neisha, Nurse Emily, Nurse Quimesha, Occupational Therapist Sheridan, Nurse Carli, Nurse Carly, Nurse Edie, Nurse Juanita, Nurse Annabella, Nurse Eliza, Nurse James, Nurse Dorothy, Nurse Miquelina, Nurse Kris, Nurse Wangari, Nurse Maya, Nurse Scotty, Nurse Annabella, Nurse Jenny, and the many other dedicated staff members that contributed greatly to my time and healing at Select Specialties Hospital, Oklahoma City.

I am grateful for the staff at Epworth Skilled Nursing. We had only a brief time together, but while I was there I received excellent care.

I am grateful for Dr. Lee, Nurse Dianna, Nurse Nicole, Nurse Dennis, Nurse Ghano, Nurse Nikki, Nurse Wendy, Tech Kaitlyn, Tech Jenna, Nurse Lacey, Nurse Mary, Nurse Emily, Nurse Brandie, Nurse Sam, Nurse Kamille, Nurse Mary, and all the staff members at Mercy ICU for the great job stabilizing me at a very scary time.

I am grateful for Dr. Wolf, Dr. Khan (again!), Dr. Sanullah, Dr. Kolli, Dr. Sheikh, Nurse Pat, Nurse Kimesha, Respiratory Therapist Lori, Nurse JoLynn, Tech India, Speech Therapist Jamie, Nurse Adrian, Nurse Lauren, Nurse Veroni, Tech Cassic, Nurse Veroni, Nurse Elizabeth, Tech Logan, Nurse Sarah, Nurse Emma, and all the staff at AMG Specialty hospital for two weeks of excellent care.

I am grateful for Dr. Tu, Nurse Tracie, Physical Therapist Justin, Physical Therapist Tori, Occupational Therapist Allison, Physical Therapist Kelsey, Respiratory Therapist Joel, Nurse Taylor, Nurse Jessica, Tech Jayla, Respiratory Therapist Sandra, Nurse Practitioner Wendy, Respiratory Therapist Sandra, Nurse Cheryl, Nurse Megan, Nurse Leslie, Nurse Practitioner Chris, Nurse Hailey, Nurse Tammy, Nurse Miranda, Nurse Robin, Nurse Jenny, Nurse Sarah, Nurse Faye, Nurse Melvina, Nurse Ashley, Nurse Kayla, Nurse Kami, Nurse Tiffany, Nurse Mel, Nurse Dani, Nurse, Occupational Therapist Assistant Kelsey, and the whole staff at Anadarko Physicians Hospital for taking me to the final step to get back home!

I am grateful for the loving people of First Baptist Church, Tecumseh, for all the prayers, cards, food, donations, visits, and lawn mowing and yard work at our home. You folks are the best!

I am grateful for the members of our community who also supported us during my hospital stay and even after we came home.

I am grateful to the dedicated people at Action Physical Therapy in Tecumseh, Oklahoma, Dr. Katy McMahan, Megan Radunzel, Lisa Estell, Caitlyn Horn, Kyle Townsend, and Receptionist Barbi Collier.

I am grateful to Gayla Higgins, English Teacher Extraordinaire for proof reading all my goofs in the original manuscript.

I am grateful for Andrew Martin of Mulplyze Global who mentored me through the process of getting our story published. I am grateful to the good people at Cedar Gate Publishing for making my dream and God-given assignment to get this book published.

I am grateful for the army of prayer warriors, in state, out of state, and out of the country, who consistently lifted us up in prayer throughout our trying journey.

I am grateful for our family who hung in there with us through thick and thin (and it got pretty thin at times) loving and praying me back into good health.

I am grateful for the best wife and life partner I could ever dream of having. Your love, encouragement, scoldings when I needed them, prayers including those at my bedside when it looked like I wasn't going to make it, timeless and tireless efforts to be with me, teaching school, and holding down our home through what must have been the most trying season of your life.

And I am grateful for our amazing, wonderful, and mighty God. From the time I gave You my heart and life when I was a young boy right up until this very moment You have never left me or forsaken me. You are so great and I am so grateful!

Made in the USA
Coppell, TX
19 February 2023

13075257R00134